D1244093

Codfish, Cats, and Civilization

by

GARY WEBSTER

(Webb Black Garrison)

KENNIKAT PRESS
Port Washington, N. Y./London

CODFISH, CATS, AND CIVILIZATION

Reissued in 1971 by Kennikat Press by arrangement
Library of Congress Catalog Card No: 77-120898
ISBN 0-8046-1407-5

Manufactured by Taylor Publishing Company Dallas, Texas

ESSAY AND GENERAL LITERATURE INDEX REPRINT SERIES

TO STURGIS BATES III

Preface

T*oday's urban culture serves as a screen. It prevents our seeing that the maker of artificial satellites and intercontinental missiles is a creature whose significance cannot be assessed apart from other forms of life. It obscures recognition that assembly lines and nuclear piles are operated by an organism whose past and future are intimately connected with a vast surrounding community of other creatures.*

Man has exterminated a few species and modified a handful of others through domestication. He has fought for his existence against non-human foes, and has derived part of his own special power from canny exploitation of living colleagues.

Homo sapiens *is a late arrival upon the planetary scene. Yet he has become the most abundant large animal on our planet. His impact upon Earth's total system of organisms in relation to their environment has far exceeded that of any other creature. Yet the story of this shaper of life can be told in terms of ways his own patterns have been affected by relationships with animals, birds, insects, and fishes.*

This volume does not attempt to deal with all the myriad forms of life which have had a part in the drama of civilization. Rather, a few selected creatures are treated in some detail. Each is symbolic of many others that bear a similar relationship to humankind.

Chapters 3, 5, 9, and 11 are slightly modified from essays originally published in the Natural History *magazine of the American Museum. Special thanks are due the editors for their encouragement and release of material.*

Were it not for the hundreds of hours spent by my wife in helping to gather data and prepare the manuscript, this volume would not have come into being. My gratitude to research librarians is boundless—especially staff members of the Joint University Libraries in Nashville, Tennessee, and the St. Louis Public Library.

Contents

Preface	7
Barnyard Beasts: Strange Builders of Civilization	13
The European Starling: Country Clown with Town-House Tastes	24
Majesty in a Fur Coat	36
The Bees Who Invented Social Security	43
Unsung Empire Builder, the Mule	58
Full Circle for the Poison People	68
Storm Center of Medical Research	80
Leptinotarsa decemlineata: The Bug That Changed Its Mind	90
The Rat: Strange By-Product of Civilization	101
Curtain Call for the Buffalo	112
The Wolf: Jekyll and Hyde of the Outdoors	122

The Fly That Came to Dinner 133

Nature's Strangest Chemical: Milk 144

The Lacquered Lady Who Kills for Men 161

The Pig: Self-Propelled Packing Plant 169

The Mexican Boll Weevil: Glutton with a One-Track Mind 181

Big Bruin: Half Brother in a Shaggy Coat 192

Gadus morrhua: The Fish That Made History 203

Br'er Rabbit's Biological Blitz 213

Strange Revenge of the Flying Axman 223

That Filthy Beast, the Ape 230

Nature's Living Surgical Knife 245

Index 257

Codfish, Cats, and Civilization

Barnyard Beasts: Strange Builders of Civilization

Thirteen lanky horses were key figures in the Spanish conquest of Mexico and its fabulous wealth.

Leading less than half a thousand men on his first campaign, Hernando Cortés advanced against some 48,000 natives. They met in the Battle of Cintla on March 25, 1519. Under cannon fire, Indians wavered—but did not halt. Line after line surged forward with bows, lances, two-handed swords, darts, slings, clubs. Describing the battle years afterward, Captain Bernal Díaz del Castillo declared there were enough Indians to bury the Spanish under the dust they could have held in their hands.

Suddenly a tiny band of riders burst from a thicket, attacked the natives from behind. Warriors who had dashed forward against muskets and artillery took one look at the cavalry, fled in terror. Never having seen a human mounted upon an animal, they thought horse and rider to be one—a weird four-legged adversary with the might of a god.

Perhaps the analogy is not as primitive as it appears. Familiarity with creatures of the household and herd has blinded us to the fact that they are beasts of destiny—shrouded in mystery, marvelous beyond the comprehension of those whom they have helped elevate from creaturehood to manhood.

Even in the industrial age, we would be neither well fed nor comfortable without the aid of our dumb allies. Only a few U.S. assembly lines turn out goods three shifts a day, thirty days a month. All 650,000,000 of the nation's cattle, sheep, hogs, and chickens are working for us on a round-the-clock basis. During centuries of pre-industrial culture, human dependence upon domestic animals was all but absolute.

When were these strange associations formed—and where? What unseen bonds tie man and his creatures together? How was the union formed? Some of these questions can be answered with reasonable precision. Others are unsolved riddles at whose secrets we can only guess.

Analysts are surprisingly near agreement concerning the epoch in which man took possession of most major animals.

Until about 10,000 years ago it is unlikely that any group of humans had won control of any creature except the dog. Beginning about 8000 B.C. there was a feverish period of domestication in three or four widely separated centers. This wave reached a peak within twenty centuries, ebbed slowly for another thirty.

Activity stopped 2000 years before Moses led his followers into Canaan. Except for laboratory animals, not one important species has been mastered in the past 4000 years. Domestication stopped as abruptly as it had started.

Abundant evidence suggests that the dog was man's first dumb ally. Its bones are common in camp sites of the late Stone Age. No other household creature even approaches it in geographical distribution, which is virtually global. Long considered to be a descendant from the coyote, many zoologists now think the dog sprang from more primitive wolf stock. Modern types, from the great Dane to the French poodle, are believed to stem from a single ancestral stock, whose early home may have been Southwest Asia.

Debate rages over the precise order in which other animals were brought into partnership with man. A stalwart long-horned ox may have been first to follow the dog. About the same period, or shortly afterward, the pig was domesticated. Householders of Egypt and Sumer, who built cities before 3000 B.C., kept large numbers of cattle, sheep, asses, swine, water buffaloes, and fowl. Ancestors of the barnyard turkey were kept by the Incas of Mexico, while the guinea fowl was already old when Roman swordsmen mastered the world.

Horses joined the barnyard circle comparatively late. They may have been domesticated by savage tribesmen who roamed the steppes of Turkestan. If so, they were probably used for several centuries before touching the fringes of major civilizations.

Consternation reigned when mounted invaders swept through valleys of the Tigris and Euphrates rivers, about 2000 B.C. Never having seen men ride upon the backs of animals, slaves and kings alike were filled with awe. Their tales probably inspired Greek legends of the centaur—a mythical creature who was half horse and half man.

Chickens, llamas, and alpacas are thought to have followed the horse. Since their mastery about 2000 B.C., no significant species has been added to the herds or flocks of any people.

Instead of being scattered through the whole cultural history of man, mastery of animals seems to have been confined to a single epoch of about 5000 years. Geographical distribution was equally limited. Far from a world-wide experiment, domestication probably developed in five centers. From them, the use of animals slowly fanned out over the rest of the globe.

Northern Europe contributed only one species—the reindeer. Africa's enormous number and variety of animals has yielded just two domestic types: the ass and the cat. Indochina was the original home of the water buffalo, zebu, chicken, and once important elephant. South America furnished man with the llama, alpaca, turkey, and guinea pig.

Southwestern Asia was the real center of major success. Here, early tribesmen mastered cattle, sheep, swine, goats, camels, and horses. It may or may not be significant that each of these creatures except the camel has hoofs, and that all can be kept in herds. It is startling to recognize that this brief list includes every animal that has made a major contribution to the main stream of Western civilization.

Domesticated in a few spots within a comparatively brief period, both the animals and their new masters began to undergo radical changes.

Some of the most obvious have been modifications in the total population of animals. Wild creatures tend to reach a natural balance, in which numbers of each species remain relatively constant. Barring some major change in the environment, all animals will approximately perpetuate themselves.

Domestication of selected animals—plus prowess in hunting—has made man a disruptive, even explosive, factor. Nature's balance has been radically changed. In the wild state, there are multitudes of species and comparatively few representatives of most types. Under domestication, man produces enormous numbers of a few species. Barnyard creatures have multiplied at the expense of other types. Consequently, our nation has 55,000,000 hogs and only a few thousand bison, 450,000,000 chickens and not one passenger pigeon.

There have been major transformations in physical traits of once wild creatures. Even without scientific breeding, animals which reproduce in captivity are quickly modified. Fed and guarded by man, they are relieved of searching for food and defending themselves. Such weapons as horns tend to shrink or disappear. Features which are prized by their keepers are likely to become increasingly prominent. Crossbreeding, whether accidental or intentional, may produce fresh traits.

Most qualities which we value in domestic animals have been produced by centuries of breeding.

Wild sheep have no wool—only fine down scattered through coarse hair. Egyptian sheep of 3500 B.C. still had manes and standing ears; the female had not yet lost her horns. These animals had coats of hair, rather than woolly fleece—though wool-bearing varieties had already developed in Mesopotamia.

Jungle fowl do not grow huge breasts or lay eggs day after day. Under man's guiding hand, their descendants in the chicken pen have become almost as highly specialized as the bulldog, greyhound, and St. Bernard. No early horse could even approach the record-breaking speed of Equipoise, nor could primitive cows match the milk production of a prize-winning Jersey. Indeed, female cattle of a pioneer herd gave only enough milk to satisfy their calves during infancy.

Even meat could be secured more easily by hunting than by guarding bony, ill-tempered cattle.

Since early livestock furnished none of the familiar products of modern herds, no one knows just why man adopted the practice of tending animals. There are three major theories.

Many analysts think domestication was accidental—arising from the keeping of pets. Men of all cultures enjoy taming creatures which range from deer to lizards. Baby animals are often treated precisely like members of the family. Among primitives it is not unusual for a nursing mother to suckle a puppy, kid, or young pig.

Practically all animals can be tamed. Algonquin Indians made pets of moose and bears. Africans have tamed even lions and leopards. Modern zoos are likely to include dozens of bizarre creatures that are tame or nearly so. But few animals breed in captivity. Even after centuries of association with man, both elephants and cats resist control of mating.

It is possible, say supporters of the pet theory, that all domestic animals stem from those pets which happened to be so constituted that they reproduced freely in captivity. According to this view, man originally expected nothing other than pleasure from the animals he kept.

Religious motives were far more important than desire for pleasure from pets, say some scholars. It is significant that strong religious feelings still attach to many domestic animals. Christianity excepted, every major religious movement either values one or more creatures for ritual use or makes an animal and its products taboo.

Indo-Europeans probably sacrificed horses long before they used them for transport. Many modern primitives keep fowl but never eat their eggs or flesh. Their sole use is in sacred rites: dissected in ceremonial fashion, they are thought to reveal clues to the future. Cats, never of economic significance in any culture, were domesticated in Egypt—where they were long considered to be sacred.

It was a flock of sacred white geese which warned Rome of attack in 390 B.C. Use of swine for food, or refusal to eat their flesh, is linked with religious sanction or prohibition.

Herds kept by early Babylonians and Egyptians seem to have served no economic purpose whatever—though the animals were reared in substantial numbers.

Even a culture's attitude toward dairy products is likely to be founded upon religious teachings. Neither the Chinese nor the Japanese have ever milked any animal—though they have kept several milk producers. Egyptians had bred special types of dairy cows as early as 2000 B.C. Peoples who use milk have shown remarkable skill in developing sources of supply. In addition to cows, there has been extensive use of milk from the goat, sheep, reindeer, camel, water buffalo, yak, zebu, horse—and even the ass.

Archaeologists have discovered ancient burial mounds in which animals were buried whole—presumably for ceremonial reasons. Various sites have yielded bones of cattle, sheep, swine, goats, and horses interred in such fashion.

Perhaps those animals which proved suitable for domestication became especially sacred as civilization developed—or perhaps ancients made determined and successful attempts to keep some of the beasts whom they considered to be linked with the divine. It is impossible to determine just what part religion played in the drama of domestication, but its influence cannot be ignored.

Still another factor may have operated to drive men and animals together. Southwestern Asia, chief center of domestication, was comparatively arid for many centuries. Yet there was sufficient rainfall to support grassy plains in areas that are now deserts.

A slight reduction in the annual supply of moisture, beginning some 10,000 years ago, doubtless had a profound effect upon all forms of life in the area. As grass began to disappear, the land was unable to support its former quota of animals. A surplus population of many species resulted.

Sharing fertile belts which gradually grew smaller, men and animals could have been forced into closer association. Taking advantage of skill in controlling the supply of food and water, men gained mastery of wild species—some of whom bred in captivity and developed domestic strains.

Considerable support for this view comes from the fact that all the important animals mastered in the cradle of civilization were grass eaters. It has also been suggested that dogs attached themselves to men in order to feast on scraps from the hunt, that wild cats retreated into Egyptian villages at each overflow of the Nile and gradually came to prefer household life to foraging for their own food.

Perhaps there is a degree of validity in each theory. Several complex factors, rather than a single simple one, may have led men and animals to associate with one another.

No matter what forces contributed to the establishment of mutual bonds, there remains another major riddle. There is no satisfactory explanation for the fact that all man's efforts have resulted in domestication of only a handful of species. Our planet teems with at least a million forms of animal life; less than half a hundred have been domesticated. Species which have been central in economic affairs of civilized man can be counted upon one's fingers.

This is not because of lack of effort on man's part. Dozens of species have been kept as household pets, exhibited in menageries and zoos. Numerous sustained attempts at full domestication have ended in failure.

After their amazing success with a few creatures, ancient Egyptians tried to extend their domination of animals. Herds of antelopes and gazelles were guarded in pastures—even in stalls. There were attempts to domesticate such varied types as the hyena, addax, and oryx. Sumerian herdsmen even tried to master the leopard.

All these experiments came to nothing—as have others in modern times. Bison, caribou, and American reindeer have resisted all man's wiles. So have the zebra, chamois, and ibex. Lines of kinship apparently mean little; though bison have been hybridized with ordinary cattle, they refuse to join the ranks of livestock. So does the peccary, a cousin of the pig. Though there are hundreds of finches, only the canary willingly forms a partnership with man. Why this should be the case, no one knows.

Sir Francis Galton, pioneer student of heredity, pondered the riddle. He solemnly concluded that domestication reached its practical limits long ago. All animals, he suggested, may be divided into two groups: those which can be domesticated, and those which can't.

Evidence in support of that conclusion is all but overwhelming. If it is correct, importance of man's role in the process is not nearly so great as it appears at first look. Powerless to make radical changes in the basic nature of wild creatures, man has been able to master only those few which have suitable traits. Domestication is less a dramatic victory of man than a signpost pointing to the possibility that a score of species developed especially for man's use.

Whether one attributes our domestic animals to providence or to chance, their contributions to mankind have been beyond measurement.

Animals constituted man's first reserve of meat, available to be killed when needed. Inventive genius later led to keeping one's capital unexpended and feasting on the interest—milk and eggs. Dung made fine fuel in areas where wood was scarce. Skins and wool provided clothing, while needles and thread were made from bones and sinews.

But the revolution that really shook ancient society occurred the day some herdsman first thought of multiplying his muscle power through the work of an animal. When and where this idea was born, no one knows. It is generally believed that oxen were used for pulling sleds and plows long before anyone thought of mounting an animal's back.

Hunting, agriculture, war, and travel were transformed by man's exploitation of brute resources. Lacking the surplus made possible by the labor of animals, it is doubtful that early cultures could have expanded.

Startling as this proposal seems, it has strong support from contrasts between progress in the Old World and the New. Both were early centers of civilization. Great cities were built in Peru and Mexico, just as in Babylon and Egypt. Incas developed astronomy and mathematics to at least the level achieved by the engineers who built the Pyramids.

There was no lack of intelligence on the part of native Americans. But neither south nor north of the equator did Westerners have domestic animals to match those of the Old World. South American beasts of burden were the clumsy, ill-tempered llama and alpaca—unable to carry more than a hundred pounds. North Americans had the idea of using animals for transportation, for Plains Indians hitched their dogs to crude sleds. But the New World had no creature to match the horse, ox, ass, camel, water buffalo, or elephant. No domestic animal of the hemisphere was sturdy enough to pull plows or wagons.

Differences in animals used for food and clothing were equally striking. Easterners were fat from the produce of cattle, sheep, hogs, ducks, geese, chickens, pigeons, horses, camels, oxen, and goats. Westerners had only the guinea pig, mallard duck, and turkey. North of Mexico, few American Indians had any domestic animal other than the dog.

Hence it may not be too extreme a view to suggest that "the birthplace of ideas" was that area in which man happened to have suitable beasts with which to pull civilization forward.

Neither this nor any other puzzle of domestication can be solved with finality. We do not know why a few species should yield to man when most defy him. Nor is there anything like complete understanding of the fact that after tens of thousands of years without them, man suddenly domesticated all the major farm animals.

Other puzzles are linked with the fact that the process of domestication was virtually completed before the beginning of recorded history. Does civilized man lack capacity to master other species—or did his ancestors really win all that will ever be significant? Does man deserve full credit for domestication—or has he simply utilized those raw materials which were already at his disposal?

Answers to these questions will not be reached until there is much more data from zoology, anatomy, psychology, geography, history, and archaeology. Perhaps answers will never be tied in neat little bundles. Without understanding those chains of events which gave them to us, we can pay tribute to our strange and wonderful barnyard beasts—builders of civilization.

The European Starling: Country Clown with Town-House Tastes

Typical farm boys who move to the nearest city are sure targets for ridicule as "country come to town." But in the case of the European starling, all the jokes are on the city slickers.

A flying vagabond with hayseeds in his feathers, *Sturnus vulgaris* has moved to the city as a sort of commuter-in-reverse. His two-legged neighbors have leaned over backward dropping hints that he isn't welcome. Instead of taking offense and leaving in a huff, he has claimed squatter's rights in dozens of downtown districts. Once a group of starlings literally stopped the clock: by perching on the minute hand of London's Big Ben. Now their mates are rumored to be planning a campaign for voting rights.

Shakespeare is partly responsible for some phases of the invasion that Britishers term "sticky" and Yankees grimly brand as "downright messy."

A relative of India's talkative mynas, the starling has a quick tongue of his own. Caged specimens, taught tunes and conversation, have been favorite pets for centuries. Only parrots and canaries are exhibited in greater numbers. Samuel Pepys's diary entry for March 1, 1668, refers to "a starling which do whistle and talk the most and best that ever I heard anything in my life." And in *I Henry IV*, Shakespeare has a character announce: "I'll have a starling shall be taught to speake nothing but 'Mortimer.'"

That did it. Global impact of that sentence is without parallel in natural history. Had he been given the slightest inkling of his pen's effect upon New York and Washington, Springfield and St. Louis, there's no doubt that Shakespeare would have substituted a parrot for that starling even if it put a limp into his lines. But he didn't foresee the ardor of Eugene Schieffelin.

This doughty fellow had two passions: birds and Shakespeare. An immigrant who made a fortune in drug manufacture, the New Yorker had money to indulge his whims. So he established the American Acclimatization Society with the goal of introducing into the New World all the British birds mentioned by Shakespeare.

He would transform Central Park into a bit of old Nottinghamshire, he promised.

Bird introduction was not a new idea. Some settlers practiced it because they wanted old-country touches about them in new lands. Others were primarily interested in experimenting with lending a helping hand to nature.

Captain Cook took barnyard fowl to New Zealand on his voyage of 1773. Five separate societies were later formed by settlers on the island; by 1906 they had successfully introduced such varied birds as the magpie, pheasant, blackbird, starling, skylark, hedge sparrow, and goldfinch.

U.S. zealots were less successful—partly, perhaps, because population pressure of native birds was such that newcomers had a hard time getting a foothold. Cincinnati naturalists spent $9000 in two years; 3000 birds of twenty species were introduced. All languished and failed. Thirty species of song-birds were freed in Portland, Oregon, without permanent effect.

It was natural for homesick bird lovers to want their adopted land to enjoy so beautiful a bird as the starling. Its summer coat of green, blue, and purple makes it one of the most dashing fellows of the British Isles. Walking briskly, instead of hopping in the fashion of most birds, his lemon beak sets off the metallic luster of breast and wings. Typical males grow to about eight and a half inches in length, with a five-inch wingspread that permits steady flight at forty miles an hour.

Strong and handsome, this much-admired bird languished every time specimens were brought overseas. More than a dozen attempted introductions failed in Ohio, Canada, and Massachusetts in the decade that followed 1875. Undismayed by the record of death, Schieffelin decided he'd try a substantial number of the birds rather than the conventional half dozen. So he brought forty pairs of starlings from England and liberated them in Central Park just before mating time 1890.

Officers of the American Museum of Natural History were soon in a dither. For the curator discovered under eaves of the building the first known U.S. nest of a starling.

Eugene Schieffelin was hugely pleased. Money he had spent on other birds was wasted. One after another his colonies had died out: song thrushes, chaffinches, skylarks, and nightingales survived only a season or two. Now there was reason to hope that America would enjoy at least one of Shakespeare's birds. Perhaps the starling would make up for the failure of less sturdy singers.

Early spread of the imported bird proved much less than spectacular, though. By the turn of the century, most residents of New York and Brooklyn had seen a few specimens. An occasional straggler was reported in newspapers as distant as Norwalk, Connecticut, and Bayonne, New Jersey. A veteran bird watcher of upstate New York got the thrill of a lifetime in 1920. Handed a strange bird killed by a farmer, he was able to identify it as a genuine starling!

Manhattan residents were not so enthusiastic. Already, a few folk were muttering that the growing size of starling roosts might someday create a nuisance. Occasionally a late-working executive was constrained to cover himself with a newspaper as he left his office. Visitors to the city snickered at such goings on; New York could have these birds.

A few decades proved that the largest city on the continent was too small to hold her feathered colonies. Population build-up pushed starlings along shore lines, first as stragglers and then in flocks. Once entrenched, they began spreading into the interior. Ohio, first known outpost west of the Alleghenies, became starling territory in 1916. Illinois and Kentucky were reached in 1920. Three years later, large flocks appeared in the nation's capital, quickly took over roosts established by purple grackles. Madison County, Indiana, was invaded in 1927, when big flues of Anderson School were seized as roosting places.

Utah was infiltrated in 1935; Colorado was reached in 1938. Just three years later, flocks were so numerous in Denver that newspapers begged for public action. Less than half a century after they began venturing from New York, starlings were well intrenched in much of southern Canada and throughout the United States except for a narrow strip of California. Mid-century estimates of population range above

50,000,000—one bird for every urban acre on the continent, and hordes of new babies every season.

These developments would delight nature lovers and please the general public were it not for one set of factors. Aside from its roosting habits, the brilliantly colored starling is a very nice fellow. He makes a good husband—even helping to hatch his mate's eggs and bringing flowers to her while she takes her turn sitting on them.

"Astute and civil," according to editorial writers of the London *Times*, this "bird of uncanny gifts" is a pleasant rustic who has entered urban life slightly out of step. A born jokester with unmatched skill as an imitator, the starling repeats almost any sounds of its immediate environment.

Botanist H. A. Allard vows that a pet bird, whom he fed in order to observe its mimicry, learned the long, low call of a flicker. As though that wasn't enough, the cutup then drummed with his beak on top of a box in imitation of the flicker's tattoo.

In cities, a starling's cry may mimic the mewing of a cat, creaking of a garden-door hinge, or calling of a nurse for wandering children. London birds who lived near hotels and theaters in days of the horse-drawn hack were even skilled in repeating the doorman's long-drawn whistling for a cab.

Despite its keen ears, the starling is seldom ruffled by roar of traffic, and pays no attention to neon lights. Superbly equipped for life as a commuter, all winter it goes about the business in reverse style by feeding daily in the suburbs and flying to downtown regions each night.

Such patterns have been adopted during the twentieth century. So long as the bird was a country dweller, roosts were usually remote from the haunts of men. A spinney of laurels, reed bed, or plantation of hawthorn might shelter as many as 250,000 birds. But a district of 100,000 square miles would include no more than ten such sites.

Without giving up its social ways, the starling has learned that heated city buildings make better roosts than icy canebrakes. So, in England as well as the United States, hordes spend their winter nights on ledges, cornices, and window sills. More than one flock has taken possession of a theater marquee—roosting on the electric lights for greater warmth.

Architects of the late nineteenth century played into the birds' hands. For museums, courthouses, and post offices of that epoch couldn't have made better roosting places if they'd been designed for the purpose. Deep archways and elaborate capitals provide ideal shelter, so that as many as 100,000 starlings can gather sociably on a single edifice. County-seat towns and state capitals naturally attract their quotas. But public buildings of the nation's capital are an easy first in starling appeal. Winter population of Washington is estimated at 4,000,000 birds, and mounts every year.

It wouldn't be a source of public concern if the starling were a more considerate neighbor. As it is, he dumps his droppings wherever the mood strikes him and chatters at all hours. After flocks arrive at the National Gallery or Metropolitan Museum, an umbrella is standard equipment for evening visitors. Puzzled by evidence of stress, maintenance men at the Illinois state capitol checked the roof, found it sagged under 22,000 pounds of droppings.

Noise is almost as big a nuisance factor. Typical feeding grounds are fifteen to thirty miles from a downtown roost. Late afternoon flocks, numbering tens of thousands, like to gather above a city in loose formation. Eddying and billowing like a cloud, birds make a sudden downrush that echoes like the roar of breakers crashing on a rocky cliff.

That outburst is simply a prelude for hours of evening chatter. No one knows what they say to one another, but roosting starlings seem incapable of keeping their mouths shut.

Given as few as, say, 25,000 birds who have seized a park in a quiet residential district, incessant conversation can drive human neighbors to distraction. Big flocks in London sometimes make such a noise they can be heard above the roar of Charing Cross traffic. Small wonder that folk of Queen Elizabeth's day used "murmuracion" as the collective name for members of a starling colony.

Twentieth-century ingenuity, adequate for such tasks as harnessing the atom and launching artificial satellites, has proved incapable of circumventing the country bird in his assault upon our cities.

Poisoning is ineffective. Few starlings will take enough of any one bait to produce fatal results. Shooting is difficult or impossible in urban centers. So most human resistance has centered in attempts at eviction from those buildings selected as roosts.

Sanitation workers of major cities have used exploding dust bags, stink bombs, soap-bubble sprays, itching powder, roman candles, aluminum owls with phosphorescent eyes and rayon feathers, recordings of starling distress calls, blinking lights, nets, and spray from fire hoses. So far, Washington officials have balked at trying the scheme used by John Messmer, building superintendent of the Milwaukee courthouse. Since many birds perched on cast iron window grilles, Messmer smeared them with axle grease in the hope that starlings would slip, fall, and knock out their own brains.

Even when early trials have given promising results, no counterattack has had lasting effect. There is a degree of irony in success. For the most effective methods of evicting these unwanted tenants have had results like those achieved in Shreveport, Louisiana. Twenty-eight live oaks in the courthouse square harbored so many starlings that the police jury authorized routing them by squads of noisemakers. After five nights, most birds were gone—seven miles east, to hangars at Barksdale Field. If driven from familiar haunts in major cities, they casually settle on a new roost a few blocks away.

Strangely human qualities of the bird contribute to both its biological success and its role as a chief feathered pest. Intelligent and versatile, starlings give such good care to their young that survival rates are high. Like men, they thrive under a wide variety of conditions instead of refusing to leave a narrow life zone. Family and group patterns not only give social stability; they also afford mass support for individual birds.

Brain weight of the white pelican accounts for only .55 per cent of its body mass, while the ptarmigan's quota of gray matter is even less. Magnificent brains of starlings make up 3.2 per cent of their total weight—a near high among birds.

This factor is believed linked with the capacity to learn calls of other birds. Visiting a rural district of England, bird watchers can listen to a starling for half an hour and list the notes it imitates to make a reasonably complete catalogue of all birds resident in the neighborhood. Individual mimics have ranges that include such diverse sounds as the clucking of a fowl, whistle of the pewee, caw of a crow, melodious whistle of the redshank, and "churring" call of the partridge.

In 1945, a Toronto starling with little formal training startled newsmen who had challenged its owner's claims. "Naughty to do it," the bird told them. Then he whistled three lines of "Home on the Range" and informed his visitors, "You're crazy."

English fancier T. H. Ferrar began systematic training of a fine eight-week bird, devoted four years to the task. His starling could mimic both the canary and the robin, speak more than a dozen short sentences with proper British accent, whistle "Pop goes the Weasel" plus an assortment of music-hall tunes.

That kind of showmanship counts for little in the struggle for food and nesting places—but throws light on some exploits of the bird so recently established in North America. There's every reason to believe that the rapid spread over the continent is partly due to nesting, feeding, and migration practices learned from native birds.

Early immigrants were year-round residents of Manhattan and environs, showed no tendency to migrate. By 1925, seasonal changes of residence were showing a strong pattern. Migration was nearly always in company with grackles, blackbirds, or robins. This doesn't constitute proof—but gives strong support to the theory that the starling who can travel or leave it alone kept a sharp eye on feathered neighbors and adopted some of their ways. Now it is not unusual for flocks to winter in Ohio or Tennessee, nest in southern Canada.

April is the typical nesting season. Starlings whose lives have been spent in rural Europe prefer to spread their sticks, straw, and feathers in some natural hole. Rocky cliffs seem to be the natural habitat of the species at the time of rearing their families.

Hardy settlers in the New World have shown their pioneer spirit by nesting in regions that offer no traditional shelters. U.S. starlings lay their eggs in steeples and cupolas, bridges and trestles. They take over deserted rabbit holes, oust woodpeckers and flickers in order to seize their nests. Thriving families have been reared in airplane hangars, pipework of television towers, and inside air-conditioning units.

Part of this versatility may be linked with the fact that it is the bold unmated cock who actually constructs the nest. Once he has tossed together a house to which he may bring a mate, courtship proceeds rapidly. Sometimes the hen takes the initiative. Sidling along a branch, she flickers her tail incessantly as she nears the gallant of her choice. If he takes to the air, she pursues him.

As the denouement of such a romance, the cock takes his turn sitting on five or six pale blue eggs laid by his bride. America's lengthy season of warm weather permits these versatile parents to rear two broods each year, instead of the single brood typical in Europe.

Many birds and animals have narrow food preferences, languish if they can't get specific items eaten by their ancestors for thousands of generations. Most martins and swallows, for example, starve if the supply of flying insects is exhausted.

Starlings actually prefer insects, too. They're inordinately fond of weevils, spiders, centipedes, and wood lice. Young ones not yet introduced to ways of the city are likely to wheel and glide, hawking for high-flying insects in the fashion of a swallow. As late as 1865, English naturalists concluded that the twelve-month diet of the starling is almost entirely insects. "They are not fond of grain," an official report said. "Fruit does not form an important item of diet in the native habitat."

Less than a century later, city-roosting birds catch only enough insects to make up 42 per cent of their diet. Cultivated fruit provides more than one fourth of it, and garbage accounts for about 20 per cent. Hungry starlings gobble potatoes, acorns, roots, snails, and even lizards. In seasons of scarcity, flocks have been seen to light on clumps of trees and strip them of leaves. Nearly all native U.S. birds refuse to touch monarch butterflies, presumably because of the noxious oil they secrete; starlings feast on them.

Even such pests as the Japanese and potato beetles are included on the menu of the bird willing to eat anything at hand. This factor explains why early studies usually ended by giving somewhat grudging commendation to the European immigrant. "It has few equals among the bird population of the northeastern United States as a destroyer of terrestrial insects," said a 1921 report based on study of 2466 stomachs.

Much evidence suggests that flexible food habits played a big part in fostering an increase of the starling population. In turn, new hordes of hungry birds began eating from back yards and dump heaps. Bonds were greatly strengthened between species by the thoughtfulness of two-legged creatures who provided huge shelters for roosting. Having taken up city ways, the starling doesn't intend to thin his ranks by a return to rural life.

As a wild bird, he is fastidious. Both cock and hen are careful to take droppings from the nest nearly every time food is brought to their young—fifteen or twenty times an hour for three weeks.

So long as rural England was its favorite haunt, an evening bath was the order of the day even in severe weather. A veteran naturalist who watched this operation many times described it as "no hurried wash, but a wholehearted and complete immersion." Lacking toilet facilities, feathered citizens of cities have learned to endure their own rank skin oil —which may be as offensive to fastidious starlings as to humans.

Highly favored by farm folk so long as its numbers are not great, the starling becomes a problem wherever it multiplies. Introduced to Australia in the 1870s, it won initial praise for prowess in clearing sheep and cattle of their ticks. Then flocks began making winter headquarters in Sydney—with results like those familiar to citizens of Louisville and St. Louis. Much the same sequence marked the spread of the starling in New Zealand and Tasmania. Recently established in South Africa, *Sturnus vulgaris* is well on the way toward becoming the most notorious feathered pest in history.

Future developments are highly uncertain.

Until it learned to eat garbage and sewage, the starling was something of a tidbit for the table. It may have been the "blackbird" who contributed four-and-twenty representatives to the famous nursery-rhyme pie. Whether this was the case or not, many a member of the race did go into pot pies of Old England. Changed diet and abandonment of the daily bath have reduced human enthusiasm for thinning their ranks by hunting.

A distinguished architect has suggested that starlings might be brought under control by wrecking most of our public buildings, erecting new ones without roosting places. That proposal gains weight when one considers that horses had to give way to automobiles in order to put the once-dominant house sparrow into an eclipse.

Hold your horses—the chain of development was not so simple as you may be thinking. Oil dripped from crankcases into city streets and was picked up by the feet of ground-feeding sparrows. Transferred to their feathers, it was passed to eggs. This closed pores and prevented hatching, so thinned sparrow ranks.

Much the same cycle might bring starlings under control . . . if anyone could figure out how to persuade 'em to put motor oil on their eggs.

Majesty in a Fur Coat

Neither war-wealthy tycoons of industry nor blue-blooded First Families make up America's real aristocracy. The nation's cats—some in middle-class homes, others in barns and shanties, and not a few in the mansions of the very rich—really constitute the patrician class. Some estimate there are about 40,000,000 of them, but they have never been actually counted.

We swaggering humans like to think they belong to us. Actually, they never have and never will. We are the servants who provide warm homes and rich food. They are the masters, tolerating man but never bowing to him.

Just when and where the domestic cat originated no one knows. Many thousands of years ago, by a biological freak or "sport," the ancestor of all tabbies may have been born of the mating of Asiatic wildcats. This is only conjecture, at best.

An Arabian legend gives the only really plausible explanation of the origin of the cat. The patriarch Noah, so the story goes, became annoyed when rats and mice began to multiply on the ark. He tried to trap the beasts but failed. Whereupon, at his command, the lioness sneezed violently and produced the first cat!

Cats began to be guests in the homes of their two-legged fellow creatures almost 5000 years ago. Probably it was much earlier, but cat figures appear in Egyptian graves dating from 2600 B.C.

Man began early in civilized times trying to improve on nature by selective breeding of the domestic cat. But he never succeeded as he did with other animals. Special types of horses have been bred for such varied tasks as draft work, racing, and military service. Literally hundreds of widely different kinds of cattle and poultry have been produced. The breeding of dogs has become a science in itself, resulting in such special canine models as the wolfhound, the sheep dog, Pekingese, greyhound, bulldog, and Skye terrier. But puss, basking contentedly before the fire in a New England home today, is essentially the same animal that indolently accepted the homage of Egyptian priests aeons ago.

Even the few special breeds that man has produced quickly lose their distinctive features if crossbred. Such traits as blue eyes and long hair are biologically regressive and disappear unless held by selective breeding. Mate any expensive breed with an ordinary domestic cat, follow the process for two generations; and not the slightest trace of the distinguishing peculiarity will remain.

Few other domestic animals revert to the wild state so quickly and successfully as puss. Several times in history, abandoned cats have gone wild, multiplied, and become a serious source of annoyance.

In 1815, when Napoleon was about to depart for St. Helena, a resident of Chester, England, perpetrated a hoax, according to E. C. Brewer in *The Historic Notebook*. The jokester had a large supply of handbills printed and distributed, explaining that St. Helena was so overrun with rats that on a certain day an agent of the French government would buy cats. He would pay sixteen shillings for toms, ten for females, and two for kittens. On the day set, the city was filled with men, women, and children loaded with mousers.

When the hoax was discovered, a riot ensued. Four or five hundred cats were killed, but at least a thousand escaped and went wild. They became such a menace to small game and domestic poultry that a regiment of soldiers was dispatched into the forests of the region to hunt and kill them.

An obscure little island near Tahiti is said to be so overrun with cats that every attempt at colonization has failed. Rats had invaded the island after a ship was wrecked on its rocks in 1862. Soon the pests became a serious nuisance. So a French trader imported a load of 500 cats and sold them at fancy prices. Soon the felines wiped out the rats, then began eating fish and game. They multiplied rapidly and became very fierce. By 1881 the colonists had given the island over to the cats and departed.

Though cases are cited of cats dying of grief on the loss of a beloved owner, they do not usually become genuinely attached to their masters. If the family moves, puss is likely to slip away and return to her old haunts unless gradually accustomed to the new premises.

One of the most famous cases of devotion on the part of a feline occurred in the sixteenth century. Sir Henry Wyat, prominent British statesman, was arrested, thrown into a dungeon, and given no food. He would have starved had his cat not accompanied him to prison, caught pigeons, and brought them to him.

Dog lovers sometimes complain of the cat's cool independence, but American farmers say one cat is worth fifty dollars a year for the protection it gives food bins. Mohammed is said to have cut off the sleeve of his robe rather than disturb his favorite cat, Muessa, who was sleeping on it. Petrarch had his cat embalmed and placed in a niche in his apartment. And lonely spinsters are not the only persons to leave fortunes to their pets. The largest legacy ever set aside for a cat was $100,000 left to Buster, a mongrel tom, by attorney Woodbury Rand, of Boston.

Blue-blooded Americans point with great pride to an ancestor who fought in the Revolution. Many families proudly trace descent from passengers who came over on the *Mayflower* three brief centuries ago. But His Majesty the Cat is descended in an unbroken line from gods and goddesses who received the adulation of human subjects forty centuries ago —before Moses led the Children of Israel from the land of the Nile.

Worshiped as deities by the ancient Egyptians, cats lived in magnificent temples and were fed like kings. To kill a feline was a crime far more heinous than the murder of a human.

King Cambyses II, of Persia, who had no such regard for Tom, once took advantage of the place he held in the eyes of the Egyptians. When he attacked the city of Memphis, about 525 B.C., he found it strongly fortified. So he hunted up several hundred cats and used them as projectiles, hurling them into the city. Horrified at such treatment of the sacred animal, the Egyptians immediately surrendered.

At death, the cats of Egypt were embalmed and reverently stored in sacred vaults. So many were treated in this manner that in modern times the burial grounds have been extensively used as fertilizer quarries. An enterprising English firm imported 180,000 of the mummified bodies in 1895. Sold at auction in ton lots, the auctioneer used an embalmed cat as a hammer!

Such a proceeding would not have been tolerated in some

periods. Even in England the cat occupied a place of great honor for hundreds of years. When the famous Dutch scholar Erasmus visited the island kingdom in 1499, he found English earls wearing cloaks trimmed with catskin as a mark of high rank. In a letter to a friend, he mentioned the fact that the visitor to an English home was expected to kiss not only his host, hostess, and all their children, but also the family cat.

Such tokens of honor were based largely on fear. Stealthy, cruel, and cunning, the cat has represented the powers of darkness and evil since the very beginning of European civilization.

In ancient Egypt every member of the household shaved off his eyebrows when the family cat died. This was done to prevent the soul of the animal from taking possession of the bodies of its erstwhile owners. Even today, in northern Europe, peasants believe that black cats turn into devils when they reach the age of seven. A feline that serves nine masters in succession earns the right, they affirm, to carry off the soul of the ninth to hell.

Superstitious fear of cats reached its height in the Middle Ages. Even in 1662, a Scottish witch named Isobel Goudie made a sworn statement that when she and her sister wished to bewitch anyone, they changed themselves into the form of cats. Though the confession was probably secured by means of torture, it led to widespread action against cats.

Many religious festivals were concluded by throwing a sack, box, or barrel of black toms into a bonfire. Spectators collected the ashes and took them home as a means of gaining good fortune. Rural Scots roasted live cats on spits to drive out the evil spirits in them. The English varied the method by using brick ovens.

No other feature of the cat has played so important a part

in its role as have the eyes. Nature offers no easily observed counterpart for the baleful glare of an angry feline. The pupils, slit rather than circular, are capable of great dilation. Behind the retina is a special membrane, the *tapetum lucidum,* which causes the familiar weird glow of various colors when light is thrown on the eyes at night.

Ancients noticed the peculiar fascination of the eyes of the cat. Hence the semi-precious stone known as cat's-eye became the symbol of ill luck.

Dark pupils of a Siamese cat flash to ruby in near darkness and when the animal is excited. Just what process is involved, no one knows.

His Highness the Cat does not step off his pedestal and work for a living. Many domestic animals furnish food to their masters, and others perform useful services. For centuries, household dogs were made to run in treadmills and furnish power for domestic devices. The cat never has submitted and never will submit to such an indignity.

True, the cat wages war on mice and rats. But those who know Tom best believe that his motive is not only food but also the pleasure of destroying hereditary prey. For centuries there have been traps and poisons far less expensive and more efficient as destroyers of rodents than are cats. Modern poisons are actually putting Tom out of the extermination business.

But his hold on civilization will not be shaken. In countless decades of domestication, he has never for an instant relaxed his grip on his human subjects—in spite of the fact that the cat has given far less to civilization than any other domestic animal.

As a matter of fact, only two cases are known in which the cat made a real contribution to progress. It was a lanky tom, hungry after a night of prowling, who tried to catch a chicken in a pen and pulled feathers through the cracks to give Eli Whitney the idea for the cotton gin. And it was an anonymous mouser that unwillingly started Benjamin West, the great artist, on his career. He made his first brush with hairs snatched from the tail of the family cat.

Every attempt to put puss to work has failed. Just seventy-five years ago, cat lovers of Liége, Belgium, formed a society for "the improvement, mental and moral, of the domestic cat." Because felines have an unfailing sense of direction, the organization wanted to use them to carry messages in place of carrier pigeons. Preliminary experiments were made up to a distance of twenty miles, when the plan was dropped. Just what steps they took on the moral issue, history does not record.

Don't be deceived into thinking that cats ever intend to concern themselves about earning their board and keep. Work is for humans. Daintily, ever so daintily, Tom will pour his supple body on the floor after consuming a bowl of milk and a platter of liver.

Just as his long-dead ancestors blandly accepted the homage of respectful Egyptian vassals, so he permits a few caresses—not too ardent or familiar—from his two-legged subjects of the twentieth century. Then, purring solemnly, Majesty in a Fur Coat drifts off into regal slumber.

The Bees Who Invented Social Security

Honeybees entered their own technological age a great many centuries before humans. Some of the most distinctive qualities of present-day culture marked insect societies that flourished before men ceased to take shelter in caves.

Aeons before members of human families began specializing in their work, bee communities practiced strict job diversification. Their craftsmen followed elaborate techniques for chemical processing of food, which was sealed in sanitary containers and stored for future use. These activities took place in air-conditioned factory units that accommodated 20,000 or more workers.

Then as now, life cycles of bees were geared to a system of social security so all-embracing that the unit of society is the group rather than the individual. It is debatable whether this represents the greatest success or the most colossal failure among insects. No matter what view one may take on that issue, there can be no dispute concerning the fact that destinies of cities and hives, long intertwined, are now so wedded that neither can flourish without the other.

Earth's 600,000 kinds of insects include more than 10,000 close relatives of the honeybee. Nineteen out of every twenty are strictly solitary; only about 500 species have adopted ways that are more or less social.

At the bottom of the social scale are wasps that build strictly individual nests but prefer to work in the general vicinity of their kinfolk. Much more elaborate bonds mark members of yellow-jacket society. Not only are progeny of several mothers reared under a common shelter; all citizens band together to defend their nest from attackers. Bumblebees establish integrated colonies. Residing in an abandoned mouse nest or other hole, a season's brood may number several dozen co-operating insects. No such community flourishes for more than a single season, for only fertile females survive the winter.

Undisturbed by seasonal changes, small stingless bees of the tropics establish more or less permanent groups. Cells are built and stored with food on which eggs are laid. But once a youngster hatches, he is on his own to eat, grow, and mature without attention from his elders.

Honeybees are not content with such slipshod ways. Every hour of a baby's life is watched. Each act is guided by instinct-bound rules of the hive. Nurses mix formulas and feed infants on schedules more rigid than those advocated by the sternest of pediatricians. Nothing is left to chance or individual whim; social routine directs the entire career of every bee.

Carefully deposited near the end of an unsealed wax cell, the egg of a bee is like a grayish comma one sixteenth of an inch long. Always the enlarged end, from which the head of the larva will emerge, is uppermost. A tough membrane gives shape to the egg and protects it from injury.

Three days pass before the membrane bursts to release a white grub that bears no resemblance to its parents. It has neither legs, wings, nor eyes. For all practical purposes, the tiny creature is simply a stomach; all other organs are insignificant.

Utterly incapable of finding food for itself, the grub would perish within minutes were it not for patterns of action inside the hive. Almost as soon as the hungry infant emerges, a nurse bee is on hand with its first meal—a speck of liquid released from glands in the nurse's head.

From that moment, it is eat, eat, eat! Eight periods of feeding during the first sixty seconds of life . . . Five hundred meals within an hour after bursting from the egg . . .

Instead of diminishing, the rate of feeding increases as hours pass. This infant is destined to be a worker, so a diet of honey and pollen replaces glandular jelly after thirty-six hours. Growing so rapidly that it must shed its skin and develop a new one every day, the glutton crams down 10,000 separate meals in five days. More than 1500 times as large as when hatched, it opens its mouth to reveal silk glands from which come wee threads with which to wrap itself in a cocoon. While the corpulent grub fashions its own shroud, worker bees cap its cell with porous wax.

During twelve days of stillness, internal transformations proceed in complex cycles, so that when the cocoon is broken there emerges—not the blind grub who entered it, but an adult bee fully equipped to contribute to life of the hive.

After a brief period of inactivity, the insect embraces a work pattern that is as elaborate and rigid as its own life cycle. For nearly a week, every minute is filled with a single chore: feeding younger sisters with the mixture of honey and pollen that humans know as "beebread."

Internal changes are taking place meanwhile. On the sixth

day, royal jelly begins to ooze from glands of the head. This thick fluid forms the diet of all young grubs for three days, and of the queen bee throughout life. Flow of the secretion ceases when a worker bee is about two weeks old. No longer capable of serving as a nurse, the mature insect tests her wings with a few short flights.

But the law of the hive decrees that she is not yet ready to enter the air force of her society. So for an additional week or ten days she works inside the community nest. There are many chores and she must take her turn at each: receiving nectar from field bees, making wax and building cells, beating her wings to circulate air through the hive, and standing guard at its entrance.

Three to four weeks old and veteran of half a dozen jobs, the bee is ready to embrace the task that will claim the remainder of her days. Until she literally wears out her body, she will be obsessed with gathering nectar and pollen for the community stockpiles.

Every limb and organ of her body is precisely adapted for this work. Her two pairs of wings—large ones in front and small behind—are equipped with tiny hooks so that in flight they function as a unit. Whirling at the rate of 12,000 beats each minute, the wings do not move directly up and down. Rather, they function like minute propellers in a cycle that involves an upstroke followed by a move forward before coming down and backward.

Flying empty, the bee may cruise at twenty-five mph as she heads for the flowers she was born to rob. Alighting, she thrusts her tongue deep into nectar at the base of the blossom she has chosen. Because her tongue is actually a long, slender underlip rather than a flat organ confined inside her mouth, she can roll it into a tube and suck sweet juice from nooks too secluded for men to glimpse.

Stolen nectar flows into her crop—a comparatively elastic bag so big that it will store a load half as great as the bee's own weight. Body juices mingle with the sweet fluid so that the sucrose (cane sugar) of nectar is converted into levulose and dextrose. These and other chemical changes yield a heavy syrup that is rich in minerals.

While taking on her liquid cargo, the bee has crawled into scores of blossoms. Her hairy body has collected a great number of minute pollen grains. Occasionally she stops to brush herself with instruments that protrude from segments of her third pair of legs. When the pollen brush becomes clogged, hind legs are crossed in such fashion that grains from one are scraped into hairy cavities on another joint of the opposite leg. By the time the nectar-laden worker flies back to the hive at fifteen mph, both her pollen baskets are packed full of moist dust—which she pries out with a spine on the end of her middle leg.

Most flower-visiting insects come in contact with pollen only incidentally. Honeybees not only collect it as a by-product of hauling nectar; they often make special trips for pollen from blossoms that offer no sweets. The protein-rich dust is an important item of diet for larvae and young adults; hence it is gathered in quantity and stored along with honey.

Queens and workers hatch from identical eggs and eat the same food during their first three days. After that, larvae destined to become workers are fed a mixture of honey and pollen—while the queen is restricted to glandular secretions from her nurses.

Queens become much larger than workers, differ from them in several important respects. One of the most obvious is the structure of the stinging mechanism. That of the queen is curved like a scimitar and can be used many times. Worker bees have straight stingers one third as long as their bodies and equipped with a set of recurved hooks near the tips. These barbs cling in the flesh of a victim in such fashion that they cannot be withdrawn. Any attempt to retrieve her weapon bursts the abdomen of the worker—for whom it is therefore suicide to sting.

Full sisters whose growth patterns vary because of controlled diets, queen and worker are functionally distinct. Much of the queen's body is filled by her big egg-producing organs—entirely lacking in the worker. But the honey crop and pollen baskets of the worker do not appear in the queen. Even the glands from which the worker produces beeswax are missing or non-functional in the case of the queen.

These differences suggest that the queen is as highly specialized for her own role as are her sisters for their task of gathering nectar and pollen. Such is actually the case; to a degree seldom achieved by any organism, the queen bee centers her entire career upon a single objective: the production of eggs.

In quite different fashion, the life of every male bee is also restricted. For the drone does no work in the hive or outside it. He eats as much nectar as four or five workers can gather and is the only member of the colony who scatters his excrement inside the hive. Lazy, greedy, and slovenly he makes such demands upon the community that any hive with more than a few hundred drones is likely to be degenerating. Workers tolerate these parasites because they alone can contribute the male cells essential to continuing life of the social unit.

Nature offers few parallels for the grandeur and pathos of sex life among the honeybees. After an old queen has left a hive, taking with her a swarm of workers to launch a new colony, a young queen bursts from her cocoon. She is likely to destroy all other immature queens—her sisters—who could become her rivals upon maturity. When five to seven days old, she selects a bright, hot day and makes the eerie voyage that beekeepers call "the nuptial flight."

As the virgin queen spirals upward, drones from her own or nearby hives catch sight of her and speed in pursuit. It was for this moment that the male was born. He is sensitive to sights and odors that impotent workers are incapable of noting. Eyes of the drone have 26,000 facets, while those of workers are equipped with a mere 12,000. His antennae bristle with some 74,000 olfactory cavities—as opposed to the 5000 sense organs of a sister who has no challenge more difficult than that of locating nectar.

Perhaps the ardent cavalier pursues his mate by whiffing her trail in the air. Perhaps he spies her through his many-plated eyes that extend almost over the crown of his head. Perhaps both sensory systems contribute to success in the incredibly difficult task of overtaking a single wee flier who has a head start on her swarm of suitors.

Few humans have ever caught so much as a glimpse of the moment of union. Every attempt to mate queen with drone in confinement has failed. Some specialists declare that flight is essential to success, for it involves expansion of the male's big tracheal sacs and consequent change in the shape of his abdomen.

Whether that is the decisive factor or not, bees do succeed in mating while on the wing. Once he has fertilized a queen, the drone's life mission is accomplished. His abdomen is torn open and he flutters down as a casualty.

It is believed that on the marriage flight, many queens mate more than once. In any case, a single venture into the blue exhausts interest-possibilities of sex for life. Her storage sac bulging with 3,000,000 to 5,000,000 sperms, the queen will retain them—living—for her five-year reign in the hive.

Elaborate systems of muscles control the pouch that holds male cells. As the queen lays her eggs, she opens or closes the pouch at will and thereby determines the sex of her brood. Unfertilized eggs yield male insects while fertilized ones produce females who will mature as queens or workers according to the diet given larvae.

During many centuries, beekeepers spoke of the largest member of a hive as the king bee. It was not until 1609 that any scientist ventured to suggest that the king might be a queen. Dutch investigators used one of the earliest of microscopes to dissect the central figure of a colony, discovered ovaries and oviduct that proved her to be an egg-producing machine rather than a corpulent male.

During most of her life, the queen is surrounded by a dozen or more workers who continually massage her body with their long underlips. Her sole food is the royal jelly, rich in pantothenic acid, that exudes from head glands of her nurses. Far from playing the role of an actual monarch, she has less freedom than any other member of the hive. She eats and lays eggs: often 2000 to 3000 a day, actually producing eggs in excess of her own body bulk every day for an extended period. Normal egg production during the career of a queen is in the range of half a million—but may go to three times that total.

It is the social system, not the queen, that rules every member of the hive. For the price of the social security developed among bees is a rigid pattern of group action so integrated that no individual insect has significance.

Honeybees will neither mate, reproduce, nor survive in isolated pairs. A well-regulated colony in a modern beehive includes about 50,000 members—but only the productive are sheltered. Sick and injured workers are driven out of the hive to perish. Drones are tolerated so long as nectar is plentiful, but at the coming of frost they are killed or exiled.

Even the queen is expendable. If she dies or leads a swarm out of the hive, one of her daughters is fed the diet that will require her to assume her mother's role in egg production.

At the height of the working season, a strong hive may include 40,000 young insects of all types, in every stage of development. Each day 1500 larvae bite their way from brood-comb cells to join the society that produced them. Highly specialized artisans perform every task from stroking the queen to building wax cells, from gathering food to beating their wings in order to air-condition the hive.

Winter's cold is met and mastered in the same fashion as summer's heat: great numbers of co-operating insects accomplish feats that none could perform alone.

Most heat loss from a living organism is through dissipation at the body's surface. The surface area becomes proportionately greater as the bulk of the body decreases. Their small size requires all insects to be cold-blooded, with bodies approximately at air temperature when at rest. Hence winter is the dreadful foe of all species. A few survive cold weather in dormant stages, but most species are so ordered that before they die from cold, females deposit eggs where their young can emerge with the coming of spring.

Alone among insects of the temperate zone, the honeybee passes the winter in a state of activity—made possible by a group process which warms the participants. Bees cease flying about when the temperature drops to 60° F.; at 57° they begin clustering into a compact mass with a hollow center.

Only the queen remains constantly at the inner surface of the cluster. Workers gorge themselves with honey—whose 1475 calories per pound make it a heat producer that is equal to prime beef. Moving their bodies in a vigorous unceasing dance, while slowly circulating from center to rim and back again, insects maintain a constant 65° within their cluster. As outside temperatures drop, density of the mass is adjusted so that bees remain cozy even when air measures 10° below zero.

No solitary insect could survive such an ordeal. Below 50°, flight is impossible to bees. Capable of walking in temperature as low as 45°, a worker is paralyzed by cold when the thermometer dips below that point. Yet, as a member of a hive consuming honey stored the previous summer, an insect can live through winters that make furnace-warmed humans squirm and complain.

It is as social creatures, not individuals, that bees have won success in the biological war against twin enemies of hunger and cold. Naturalist Edwin Way Teale suggests that in their colonial life they exhibit "one of the great, living philosophies of the world." And he points out that they succeed in doing so despite the fact that they have neither pamphlets nor speakers, foundations nor endowments!

Such a verdict ignores the now-established conclusion that bees do have a system of communication. Karl von Frisch has convinced the scientific world that any scout who finds a new source of nectar can tell fellow workers its location by means of a complex "dance." Though details of the pattern are obscure, its general form is believed to be understood. Some movements indicate the direction of a nectar find, while others give clues as to its distance.

Human understanding of such signals is necessarily limited, for men are incapable of entering the world of bees. Apparently a built-in navigational system enables an insect to use the sun for orientation during flight. Many investigators believe bees are sensitive to infrared rays from the sun; so far, lack of suitable experimental apparatus has made it impossible to test the theory.

Numerous series of tests indicate that bees are not colorblind, as long thought. Instead, they seem to distinguish at least four different colors in the visible spectrum: yellow, blue-green, blue, and ultra-violet. They are known to be incapable of distinguishing some shades of red; this factor may be the key to a riddle propounded long ago—Europe, having long depended upon bees for much work of pollination, has comparatively few plants with crimson flowers. Invisible to bees and hence bypassed during the nectar season, perhaps such plants have gradually become extinct on that continent.

Relatively insensible to sounds that are caught by human ears, bees are highly responsive to physical vibrations. Because their antennae are densely covered by sense organs, it is believed that they live in an odor-dominated world.

Ability to distinguish faint odors may account, at least in part, for unmatched skill in finding and blending foods. When a bee has begun taking pollen or nectar from a particular type blossom, it remains faithful to that one so long as the supply lasts. Some naturalists believe this gives the bee an advantage: by visiting a succession of identical flowers, the marauder becomes familiar with their structure and saves time.

Whether this is the case or not, such a pattern of robbery has great significance for our planet's vegetation. By confining a period of activity to a single species, a bee multiplies the likelihood that pollen from its body will fertilize the flowers it visits.

Swollen with stolen sweets half as bulky as her own body, the worker bee carries a pay load of about one ten thousandth of a pound. Since nectar is concentrated in flight as well as condensed in the hive, some 40,000 loads are required for sixteen ounces of finished honey.

U. S. Department of Agriculture scientists once installed hives in an isolated region of Wyoming—eight miles from the nearest source of nectar. Flying sixteen-mile round trips, bees logged an estimated 640,000 miles for one pound of honey. Even in regions where flowers are abundant, they probably average twice around the world for every pound—which men retail for less than half a dollar.

Though nectar is the only raw material that enters honey, the finished product of the flying craftsmen is quite different from the sweet water of flowers. By the time a load reaches the hive, it is already well mixed with body juices of its insect carrier. Instead of depositing her cropful directly in a wax cell, the field bee confronts one of her younger sisters who is working inside the hive. Stroking the nectar carrier with her forefeet, the house bee takes part or all the load in her own sac. A kind of first stomach equipped with valves and muscles, this bag is so fashioned that its contents may be passed on into the digestive system—or emptied back through the mouth.

Distended from her load of fresh nectar, the house bee finds a quiet nook and begins working the fluid. She forces the nectar out on her tongue, pushes it forward and then sucks it back again. Again and again, for perhaps fifteen minutes, she repeats this action. Then she deposits the thickened fluid in a cell. Additional moisture is lost through evaporation, for hordes of bees fan their wings continuously to keep air currents circulating above the ripening honey.

Cured and sealed, honey constitutes a unique food. Nature's only finished sweet, it cannot be altered by man without detection. For when diluted with water it ferments, and when adulterated with some other type of syrup it separates.

No one knows how long it keeps in the natural state. Bits of honey dug from an Egyptian tomb after 3000 years were found to be thick and dark—but still pure and sweet.

Until recent times, the elixir of the bees was the only sweet known to civilization. Hence it was so greatly prized that beekeeping was an elaborate art at least 5000 years ago. As late as the ninth century, honey was a major enticement for adventurers who pushed into virgin forests along the Dnieper River and its tributaries. Alexander the Great was embalmed in honey. But most folk preferred to eat it, and sometimes bartered it for its weight in gold.

Modern refining methods have led to an abundant supply of cheap sugar from cane and beets. So it would seem reasonable to believe that advancing technology should render the honeybee obsolete. Until late in the last century, just such a chain of developments appeared to be taking place. But in our time, man's explosive role as a changer of life patterns has made honey production of secondary interest. Far more important is the fact that the insect who steals the flower's sweetness is also responsible for its cross-pollination.

A few specialists have ventured to make general estimates. According to them, pollination by bees is thirty to fifty times more significant than the annual 400,000,000-pound crop of commercial honey.

Most insect pollinators are highly specialized; the honeybee is practically omnivorous. Under conditions of scarcity, workers collect nectar and pollen even from such plants as oak, pine, and cypress, tomato, beet, and rye grass. Without the pollinating activity of bees, as many as 100,000 species of flowering plants might disappear from Earth.

Man's use of poisons has greatly thinned the ranks of native insects that visit commercial crops. His development of early-blooming varieties has thrown many wild pollinators off schedule so that they are incapable of functioning. And his practice of planting huge fields to a single crop has discouraged those insects that take only a few kinds of nectar from wild flowers.

Converging effects of these factors have produced a situation in which the honeybee accounts for about 80 per cent of all insect pollination in North America. Beginning with apple orchards in 1926, every subsequent year more and more rented hives have been used in commercial farming.

In the alfalfa regions of Utah, each season sees 10,000 or more colonies of bees imported for the work of pollination—after which hives are moved 500 miles back to California. Texas farmers have boosted cantaloupe crops by using bees at the rate of two hives per acre.

Experimental plots in Arizona cotton fields showed a 21 per cent boost in lint yield when bees were introduced for work with early-flowering varieties. From Bruce plums to cucumbers, an increasing number of fruits and vegetables are being grown with the help of bees. At least fifty crops are already affected, and the tempo of beekeeping is rising fast.

World population of the insect is at an all-time high—and is centered in the machine-minded Western Hemisphere. This development is precisely contrary to that in relationships between man and his only other fully domesticated insect, the silkworm. Invention of synthetic fibers has virtually put the spinner of silk out of business. But each new technological advance tends to magnify the importance of the creature whose life is devoted to robbing flowers.

First domesticated in the cradle of civilization long ago and now securely established as an essential agent in the machine age, the bee of today is aided as never before in its history.

Humans not only build strong houses in which colonies

may be sheltered; they also operate machines to make comb foundation that reduces the work of the hive. Man-made poisons decimate insects that compete with bees, while human influence has boosted ranks of the honey makers to some 300,000,000,000 in the United States alone. To top it all, men annually transport hives long distances in trucks and planes and make it increasingly easy for bees to gather their nectar.

These developments pose a somewhat baffling enigma: taking the long look at our planet and measuring biological success in terms of numbers, do men really keep bees—or do bees keep men?

Unsung Empire Builder, the Mule

Poems and statues, paintings and ballads pay tribute to the horse. His half brother, the mule, is a noble beast without whom history would be quite different. Yet few pause to recognize his central role in the drama of Western civilization. Instead of singing praises of the sturdy hybrid, those who know him best devote their talents to framing new jokes about him.

Most jibes directed at the beast focus on one of three matters. First, he is sterile—quite incapable of propagating his kind. Second, he is the offspring of a jackass (mated to a horse). Third, in season and out, he kicks with great skill and every evidence of malice aforethought.

"No wonder the mule is so ornery," runs a proverbial quip. "He's the only common animal who has neither pride of ancestry nor hope of posterity." Josh Billings, homespun humorist of the last century, put it like this: "The mule is haf hoss and haf jackass, and then kums to a full stop, natur discovering her mistake."

Youngsters of past generations learned to joke about the jar-head as though he had no redeeming qualities. "The best way to put a mule into his stall," said a standard formula, "is to hire someone else to do it." Half a hundred collections of humor included the question, "Why does Missouri stand at the head in mule raising in the United States?" "Because," ran the answer, "it would be dangerous to stand at the other end." Grandpa thought that one hilarious.

Perhaps the ancient herdsman who saw the world's first mule blinked his eyes and concluded that nature had played a joke. For even the most ardent admirer of the animal never entered him in a beauty contest. He looks just like what he is: a cross between a donkey and a horse, with all the most unattractive features of both.

Yet the ungainly fellow soon proved his special usefulness. Near Eastern breeders of pre-historic times knew the mule to be stronger than the donkey, tougher than the horse. What he loses in looks, he gains in fortitude. From his mother, the mare, he derives strength and courage. From his father, the jack, he inherits patience, sobriety, and sure-footedness.

His skin is harder and less sensitive than that of the horse. He is less impatient under heavy loads, more cautious in places of danger, less susceptible to disease. Like his father, the mule thrives on a diet so coarse that it would make a horse ill. He has the donkey's indifference to heat, the horse's capacity to pack heavy loads. As a work animal in hot regions he is magnificent.

Assyrians and Egyptians appreciated him so highly that they sometimes represented him on monuments. They used the mule as a pack animal, reserving their horses for military expeditions. Neither beast seems to have been abundant, for human labor was the chief source of energy in building the Pyramids and other great structures of the period.

Mules were still comparatively rare when David became King of Israel some 3000 years ago. His sons, the princes, were proud to have them for their personal mounts. Solomon even rode a mule when he was proclaimed King, and the high value that was placed on them is indicated by the fact that they were among the yearly presents given him during his long reign.

The people of Israel were prohibited from breeding their own mules (Leviticus 19:19). So they probably imported them from great stockyards in Armenia. Old Testament references indicate that the mule was used as a beast of burden and baggage animal in war, and he was harnessed to litters as well as ridden. Sennacherib carried off a large number of mules after he invaded and conquered Judah. Conversely, exiles who returned to that land from captivity in Babylon brought home 245 of the animals.

During this era, the hybrids were used to pull chariots in the great city of Nineveh. One monument even shows a woman of the city riding a mule. Another ancient marker depicts gay blades of Babylon riding mules to a deer hunt.

The Romans, who became masters of the known world, had a high opinion of the mule. Already breeding had become a recognized art. It was well known that mating of a stallion and a female donkey never produced a mule. Such a hybrid, vastly inferior to progeny of a male donkey and a mare, was called the *hinnus*. Centuries have modified the name but little. Still familiar to stockmen as the hinny, this animal is never intentionally reared.

Detailed knowledge of genetics is still lacking, but it appears that horse and donkey qualities are transmitted quite differently. Hybrids seem to get the size and body of the mother, whereas the feet, head, and tail appear to be most affected by the father. So a horse father and donkey mother produce a creature that most people consider all but useless, the little hinny, while a donkey father and a horse mother produce the sturdy, sure-footed mule.

Though stockmen in the time of the Caesars had no scientific explanations in terms of chromosome reactions, they were well aware of differences between *mulus* and *hinnus.* They bred the former so effectively that the Latin name was only slightly changed in transmission to English and other languages.

They had not yet formed the modern attitude of scornful contempt toward the mule. The Romans used the animal for carrying packsaddles, drawing carriages, and plowing in light soil. They even employed an enclosed chair attached to two long poles, especially designed to be slung between two mules. Passengers were wealthy and highborn ladies who could afford to ride in style.

The decline and fall of the Roman Empire caused the center of progress to shift southward. For a period of several centuries Africa threatened to regain her ancient position as hub of the civilized world. Mule breeding continued throughout this epoch. Fine hybrids were greatly prized, for governors of both Syria and Egypt sent them as gifts to the prophet Mohammed. One white mule named Duldul was accompanied by a bale of rich clothing and two Coptic slave girls. Mohammed was not especially interested in the girls but took great pride in his white mule.

Followers of the prophet invaded Europe early in the eighth century. Charles Martel and his Franks stopped their advance in 732, but the swarthy fanatics clung tenaciously to most of the region that later became Spain. They were hardly established in their new domains before they began breeding mules, for the hybrid seemed especially fitted for service in the rough mountainous country. Generations of experiment had already given Moorish stockmen great skill.

Now they produced mules with big, strong bodies—plus the slender legs and small feet of a donkey.

It was this type of mule that became the major pack and riding animal of old Catalonia. Firmly established in most of Spain, it remained behind when Europeans began to drive out the Moors in the thirteenth century.

By this time, however, the sure-footed animal was strongly linked with the hated invaders who had made such good use of it. Some even argue, in fact, that the derogatory views of the mule may stem, at least in part, from centuries of strife between horse-breeding Christians and mule-breeding Moslems.

As soon as Castile and Leon were united under one king, he tried to outlaw Spanish use of the mule. His first edict was issued soon after the capture of Seville, in 1248. According to it, the *caballero* of Spain was required to forsake use of the mule and stick to the ancient and honorable practice of riding the horse. But many a mule must have given a lusty heehaw at the royal proclamation. For even the nobility rode hybrids in preference to the clumsy, high-spirited horses then being bred.

Matters reached such a state that a special report was made to Ferdinand and Isabella, just two years after the discovery of America. According to it, the nation could muster only 10,000 or 12,000 horses for use in battle against the Moors. Meanwhile at least 100,000 subjects of the king were riding mules. Ferdinand pulled out dusty codes, ordered that only clergy and women should ride mules—on penalty of having the mounts killed.

Christopher Columbus was decidedly put out. In 1505 he asked for a special license that would permit him to ride muleback instead of horseback. His Majesty graciously granted it to the old explorer by virtue of his age and infirmities. But he made it clear that this Moorish practice was not for everyone. A few mules were actually executed at Valladolid and other towns because their owners insisted on riding them.

Adventurers and explorers in Spanish America found conditions that demanded the use of mules. Importation and breeding soon reached major proportions. For 400 years the drab and despised mule served as the most important work animal of the two continents.

It was the mule who proved hardy enough to survive the rigors of swamps, deserts, and mountains. The world's most significant pack trail at that time crossed the Isthmus of Panama from Panama City on the Pacific side to Nombre de Dios on the Atlantic. Leather, grain, meat, and other provisions were shipped west; gold and silver came east. And Nicaragua became the great center of mule raising for the isthmus trade. It was not unusual for 1500 animals to leave one of the terminal cities in a single day. Most of the loot of South America that was funneled into Panama crossed the isthmus by mule train, then went to Europe by ship. In the single month of March 1550, the Spanish hauled 1200 muleloads of gold and silver to Atlantic ports.

Inevitably privateers began to eye the situation with great interest. Sir Francis Drake heard that the mules of the isthmus packed metal bars as though they were cordwood. So he attacked a train on Valentine Day 1573. To his disgust, the Spanish had sensed trouble and sent only less important freight. Six weeks later, however, the dashing Englishman captured a valuable train of 190 mules. But he had only thirty-five Europeans in his command, and—carry what they could—they had to leave more than fifteen tons of bar silver behind.

Mule traffic along the strategic trail continued long after

the flow of precious metal was exhausted. Goods shipped to or from California could take one of two routes: the long, precarious voyage around the cape—or across Panama by mule. Consequently business boomed during the California gold rush. Mules staggered westward with miners and their gear, packed millions in gold back across the isthmus.

As late as 1852 Ulysses S. Grant and eight companies of the U. S. Fourth Infantry rode mules on one leg of the trip across Panama. Though a railroad was under construction, mule trains operated between its terminal and the coast.

Mules were a major factor in the early development of California. Pushing slowly northward from Spanish centers, the hybrids were numerous in fifteenth-century Mexico. As fast as missions were established in new territory, mules went along. Charles III of Spain decided in 1768 to settle the northwestern portion of his North American empire. So he sent a viceroy with orders to build posts in such spots as San Diego and Monterey. Starting from Lower California, the expedition gathered stock from every mission on the way. They found sixteen broken mules at the mission of San Francisco Xavier, twenty-six at San José de Cummundia. When they had accumulated more than 100 of the essential animals, along with a smaller number of horses, they moved into Upper California.

Cowboy movies to the contrary, the mule played a more significant role in the development of our West than did the more glamorous horse. Mules survived heat and poor food that no horse could endure. They reached a peak of usefulness on the Santa Fe trail, where Mexican mule skinners packed animals with loads up to 300 pounds.

Mules pulled clumsy mud wagons—light coaches similar to the army ambulance—over multitudes of trails and rough roads. Three pairs of them were hitched to the first Concord coaches that rolled west of the Mississippi. Even in 1875, more of America's freight was hauled by mule trains than by railroads.

Travel difficulties were such that it was not feasible to bring mules from the Southwest to farming regions of the East. As late as 1826, the vast sugar industry of Louisiana boasted only an occasional mule. Two or three expeditions were organized to bring herds of them from the West: one speculator bought 600 in San Francisco for the purpose. Nothing came of his other efforts.

It was a gentleman planter of Virginia who first saw that farmers of the Atlantic seaboard would have to raise their own mules. His name was George Washington.

As early as the spring of 1785 he expressed great eagerness to experiment with the hybrids. He gave his agent an order to buy "a good Jack Ass from Spain, to breed from" but found the price too high and canceled his request. King Charles III learned of his interest and shipped two animals to him as a gift. One died at sea. The other, duly received, was named Royal Gift and given a special stall on the Mount Vernon estate. On December 19, 1785, Washington wrote a formal letter of "thanks for the Jack Asses." It is still preserved in the Spanish National Archives at Madrid.

General Lafayette sent his American comrade an animal from Malta. Washington expanded his stable so rapidly that when he made his will in 1799 he disposed of forty-two working mules and fifteen younger ones.

Henry Clay brought a pure-blooded jack into Kentucky in 1832. Four years later a Dr. Davis of South Carolina imported one directly from Spain. Throughout the Southeast, plantation owners clamored for mules. These hardy animals, easy to keep and to feed, offered riches to those lucky enough to secure them. At the mid-point of the nineteenth century, U.S.

mule production was rising faster than that of any other farm animal. The total number in the nation actually doubled between 1850 and 1860.

Tens of thousands hauled ammunition, supplies, and guns in the Civil War. Observers from other nations were tremendously impressed with the stamina of the animal. Both Japan and Russia began buying mules for military purposes; England organized special mule batteries for service in border districts of India.

Peacetime uses of the animal multiplied. Spain and France produced great numbers for export—50,000 a year left the Poitou district of France alone. Brazil launched a mule-drawn express coach, with a scheduled run of 100 miles in twelve hours. An expeditionary force into Egypt rejected pleas of horse breeders, selected mules from Sicily. Missouri, Texas, Tennessee, and Kentucky jostled for leadership in the U.S. trade.

During the second half of the last century, mules literally built empires. They hauled supplies and equipment for work camps along sprawling railroad lines. Vast numbers were worked in mines; some of them spent most of their lives underground. Others pulled barges through canals, streetcars in growing cities, lumber wagons in the forests. By 1875 the mule's prestige had become so great that some of the animals were exhibited at the famous Crystal Palace show.

General Kitchener was given a special exhibition at West Point in 1910. Sixty-four Missouri mules, recently acquired, were loaded with 14,000 pounds of ammunition and supplies in just fourteen minutes. The bond between the animals and the future officers grew so strong that the mule became mascot of the West Point football squad.

In spite of mechanized conflict, mules played a strategic part in World War I. Nearly 5000 were killed with the A.E.F.

alone. From the end of the struggle until about 1925, the mule continued to increase in importance. That year, U.S. farms and industries worked nearly 6,000,000 of them.

Ever since that time, trucks and tractors have been replacing mules at an increasing rate. World War II brought a temporary revival to the trade, but interest sagged as soon as the production of machines was increased. There is no doubt about it; the hardtail is doomed.

There is something a bit pathetic about the fact that dog-food plants are now springing up most rapidly in sections where mules are most abundant. Give the patient empire builder another hundred years or so, and he will be all but extinct in the United States. Children of the future will know him only as a queer-looking specimen at the zoo.

Perhaps his stock will rise when he is no longer on hand to provoke abuse, profanity, and crude jokes. No amount of humor at his expense can alter the fact that he is the most successful hybrid that man ever developed. Bred one generation at a time for more than 3000 years, his patient labor was essential to the development of the mechanized culture that has made him obsolete.

Full Circle for the Poison People

Cobras are estimated to have claimed more human lives than World Wars I and II combined. Yet members of the strange clan whom Kipling feared as the Poison People are fast regaining their ancient reputation as guardians of life.

Venom from Old World killers is playing increasingly dramatic roles in clinics and hospitals. So today the cobra's prestige is at a level surpassed only in pre-historic cultures whose religious rites gave the serpent a permanent place on the physician's badge of office. To a degree unmatched in man's appraisal of his death-dealing competitors, the hooded reptiles have come full circle in thought.

Nearly all men in every age have regarded serpents with awe as well as fear. Even those species that are harmless—92 per cent of all snakes—evoke admiration and pose deep riddles.

At the risk of endangering his reputation for universal wisdom, King Solomon confessed that he could not comprehend the way of a serpent on a rock. Legless locomotion also puzzled the great Aristotle, who suggested that it is contrary to logic that a creature without "points" should be able to move.

Aristotle's error lay in his failure to recognize the snake's version of feet. Broad plates of abdominal skin overlap like shingles on a roof. The sharp forward edges of these plates catch against even slight projections and afford considerable purchase. Abdominal scales are linked with ribs, which are in turn attached to vertebrae. When crawling slowly, a snake flexes a few pairs of ribs and advances several rows of plates. Bracing them firmly, he pulls his body forward and then repeats the cycle. Awed by the poetry of such flowing, John Ruskin said of a gliding serpent: "It literally rows on the earth, with every scale for an oar."

The role of the snake's skin in locomotion was not understood by ancient naturalists, but they gave great attention to its periodic renewal. A thin, nearly transparent layer covers the scaly armor. This outer covering is shed at frequent intervals—not in patches like that of a beauty queen who has had too much sun, but entirely.

Two weeks before discarding its skin, a snake's colors dull. Film over the eyes becomes almost opaque. Then special glands release a potent oil that spreads between old and new layers. Persistent rubbing against the top of its head causes a break in the creature's outer case—now dead and dry. After eye plates are shed, skin is rubbed from forward edges of the lower jaw. Then the rejuvenated serpent literally crawls out of its skin—turning it inside out and discarding it like an old stocking.

Some authorities believe it was this periodic "renewal" through molting that linked serpents with immortality in ancient thought. Small wonder that seers of Egypt and Babylon should pay homage to the creature with capacity to be reborn in such fashion.

Reverence was doubtless heightened by other unique features of the serpent tribe—especially eyes and tongue. Since a transparent covering wraps the entire body, no snake can ever close its eyes. Modern investigators find this an impossible barrier in trying to determine whether or not the creatures sleep. Ancient observers, intrigued by the unblinking orb, considered it to have hypnotic power and from this belief fashioned elaborate theories about "the evil eye."

At least twenty centuries of inquiry have centered on the constantly flickering forked tongue of the snake. Scientists are still far from agreement concerning its major functions. Some support the pre-Christian theory that it serves as a decoy to hold the attention of prey. Many insist that it is an organ of touch.

Others, including the world-famous specialist Raymond L. Ditmars, have concluded that the nerve-tipped tongue is a delicate organ of hearing that compensates for the snake's lack of ears. Recent experiments challenge all these theories and suggest that the flickering tongue functions to catch and transport minute particles to a complex organ of smell in the roof of the mouth.

The earless skin-shedding creature without feet whose unblinking eyes contrast strangely with its vibrating tongue is queer enough when surveyed with scientific detachment. Add the fact that though many kinds of snakes are deadly to man in spite of the fact that all are shaped like the life-giving male organ, view through the eyes of ancient nature worshipers and it is no longer seen as strange but altogether logical that the serpent should be a major figure in world religions.

Often depicted tail in mouth to symbolize endless duration, the serpent dominates religious art of cultures that flourished in Egypt, India, Persia, Burma, Java, Ceylon, China, Japan, Mexico, and Peru. In the Bible, it is a symbol of wisdom. Egyptian worship linked the creature with Kneph, and in India it is associated with Vishnu, Siva, and Buddha. Greeks paid tribute to it as the patron or ally of Apollo, Athene, and Hermes.

The notion that snakes play a powerful or dominant role in human fertility is world-wide. Primitive cultures as diverse as those of New Guinea and Alaska still include myths about the mating of reptiles with virgins. It is in its role as a symbol of sex that the serpent beguiles Adam and Eve in the garden. Romans explained phenomenal greatness by declaring mighty leaders to be sons of serpents; this story was told of Alexander the Great, Scipio Africanus, and Augustus Caesar.

Since cobras abound in regions where the earliest civilizations flourished, it is natural that they overshadow all other reptiles in the importance of their place in thought and worship.

During many Egyptian dynasties, the most common of body ornaments was the cobra with expanded hood. Priests, nobles, and slaves alike wore cobra rings, bracelets, necklaces, and pins. King Tutankhamen, who reigned in the fourteenth century B.C., affected a royal headdress fashioned like an erect cobra and was so depicted on walls of his famous tomb at Luxor. Often mummified, especially for burial with Pharaohs and high priests, the cobra figures largely in records of state—where it is solemnly termed *ouro*, or king.

As with human rulers, so with the gods for whom they acted as regents. Figures of Isis and other divinities were given crowns shaped from intertwined cobras. Temples and shrines were decorated with the serpent symbol in many forms. In the Book of the Underworld, it is a pair of cobras carrying crowns who lead the procession in which twelve gods escort the primeval serpent Mehen to the East.

Since the Egyptian cobra is the most numerous and dangerous of the trio of poisonous snakes found in biblical lands, it may have been this creature that killed some of Moses' band. To counteract the work of his "fiery" foe, the leader of the exodus fashioned a brazen serpent and displayed it upon a pole. Six hundred years later, idolatrous folk among the Hebrews were still burning incense to the reptile—so Hezekiah destroyed the image.

Far to the East, the Naga raj (rajah, or king cobra) so captured the mind of India that it became the key figure in Hindu mythology. Even today, Shesha Nag (the thousand-headed cobra) is the basic symbol for Hindu concepts of eternity, infinity, and ultimate absorption in the great energy that sustains the universe.

A cobra was intimately involved in the emergence of Buddhism from Hinduism, for it was Naga who sheltered and supported the Buddha at the time of his enlightenment. Hence the seven-headed cobra is a central figure of Buddhism.

Greek and Roman veneration for serpents was probably linked with rites of Egypt and Phoenicia rather than the Far East. Before the time of Homer, snake cults were so well established that Zeus was described as having revolted against a serpent-deity and seized his power. As late as 200 B.C., a temple of Juno only a few miles from Rome included a cave inhabited by a cobra—to whom maidens were taken that their virginity might be tested.

Boundary lines between concepts of fertility, immortality, and health are not entirely precise even today. Ancient thought made distinctions far less clear. In wholly unconnected as well as interrelated cultures, the serpent was revered as the most potent of all healers. Hence the creature was linked with or sacred to such diverse gods of healing as Esmun in Phoenicia, Rudra in India, Ramahaualy in Polynesia, plus Isis, Harpocrates, and Serapis in Egypt.

It was Greek veneration for the serpent, transmitted through Roman culture, that gave the world its universal symbol for one who heals. Aesculapius, son of Apollo, was the first man to discover the secrets of medicine. According to early Greek lore, he learned forbidden things from a centaur.

Zeus discovered the treachery and feared that the youth would make all men immortal. Slain by a thunderbolt from the hand of Zeus, Aesculapius became the Greek god of medicine; his daughter, Hygeia, became goddess of health.

Artists commonly represent the deity of healing as standing bare-breasted, holding a club about which the serpent-god was coiled. Myths of Aesculapius had considerable influence upon the thought of both Socrates and Plato. When pestilence threatened Rome in 293 B.C., his cult was introduced to the capital city by fetching a venomous serpent for whom a great temple was built. Transmitted through all subsequent Western culture, the club and serpents of Aesculapius form the standard physician's emblem of the atomic age.

If Greeks were acquainted with cobras, it was through importation. For no species flourishes in Europe or America. Africa has about a dozen kinds—twice as many as are found in Asia.

It was a spectacular Asian variety, however, that gave rise to the now-universal common name of the reptile. Early Portuguese explorers were astonished to find snake charmers displaying their skill in the major ports of India. Snakes used for such exhibitions raise one third of the body from the ground and may remain upright for an hour or more. Distending flexible ribs of the neck, one of the angry killers displays a wide hood that shows weird markings not visible when at rest. Awed by the distinctive phenomenon, European adventurers called the creature *cobra de capello* ("snake with a hood").

Ability to spread neck ribs is not limited to cobras, though it is especially spectacular among some types of them. All snakes have flexible mouths and necks; otherwise they would be incapable of eating prey of any size.

Since the teeth of a snake are suited for puncturing but not for chewing, food must be swallowed whole. Bones of the lower jaw are loosely connected with one another and with the skull. Hence the typical serpent can capture an animal two or three times as thick as its own head, stretch jaw and ribs, and cram the quarry into its gullet.

Dietary preferences of cobras are not unusual. Like all snakes, they refuse vegetable food and thrive on frogs, mice, fish, and insects. Zoo specimens show a decided preference for the flesh of other reptiles; one exhibited by Ditmars digested 145 feet of snakes in nine months.

Except for the ringhals of Africa, all cobras lay eggs. India's spectacled type—which gave its name to the entire clan—commonly lays a batch of about twenty. Creamy-white, the tough-shelled eggs look somewhat like those of pigeons and require seven weeks to hatch.

Naga raj is the biggest member of the family, which may contribute to his receiving the title "king." Thriving throughout India, Malaya, and southern China, the king cobra is the largest of poisonous serpents. Lengths of thirteen to fifteen feet are not uncommon; one specimen reached a record eighteen feet. Fanciers regard this creature as the most beautiful of snakes, for his olive background shows markings that range from black and orange-red through yellow to ivory. Bronze eyes staring implacably, the king cobra is often listed as the most dangerous animal on earth.

His Egyptian cousin, naia haie, is comparatively dull.

Usually a medium brown with lusterless scales and seldom surpassing six feet in length, this is the cobra used by Egyptian snake charmers. Frequently referred to as the asp, it was this creature that Cleopatra probably used in her suicide. In Shakespeare's re-creation of the Egyptian queen's final hour, the rustic who brings her the instrument of death remarks that "the worm's an odd worm."

Yet it is neither the asp nor the king cobra that specialists regard as oddest in the family. Ranging from upper Egypt to the Transvaal, there is a queer "spitting cobra" with power to squirt venom into the eyes of an enemy standing six or eight feet away from him. Equipped with unique fangs whose inner holes are curved near their ends, this serpent doesn't have to bite his victims in order to inflict serious injury. Two less abundant cousins in Malaya and Africa also show specialization for chemical warfare at a distance.

Large-scale religious veneration of the cobra is now limited to Asia. Its importance on that continent is indicated by the fact that Volume One of *U. N. World* includes a description of the Nagpanchami—or ceremonial worship of the king cobra.

As witnessed by U.N. observers in the town of Wai, on the Kistna River, the fete still has many attributes of a primitive fertility rite. An image of Naga, hood expanded to strike, is a central feature of the community shrine. While priests follow centuries-old dance movements that ensure the conception of many children, villagers make offerings of plantains, roses, spiced rice, coconut, and tulsi leaves. Children conceived after homage is paid to the cobra may be given symbolic names such as Nagappa or Nagamma.

Snake worship thrives in much of rural India—from the Kashmir to the Punjab, throughout Bengal and Assam. Less common in Burma, it is still far from extinct in that exotic land. Members of a 1940 expedition actually secured, for *Life* magazine, photos of a Burmese priestess engaged in rites with a twelve-foot hamadryad (king cobra). After playing with the deadly reptile until he became tired, the woman gave him three symbolic kisses upon his head.

It is veneration for the cobra that accounts for the still-high death rate in many regions of Asia. Since one who kills a sacred reptile will be cursed with sterility, the creatures are tolerated even in dwellings. Rural folk often feed and protect the cobra who deigns to bless their household with his presence.

Small wonder that Southeast Asia is the world's worst snake-bite area. Accurate statistics are not available; most authorities settle for a general figure of 25,000 to 35,000 deaths each year. Burma's Irrawaddy and Chindwin valleys, plus India's Ganges delta and West Bengal, represent some of the most dangerous regions on earth. Yet the problem is not strictly rural; Bangkok is only slightly smaller than St. Louis —and shelters hosts of cobras in residential districts. The combined work of cobras, vipers, and kraits takes a human toll estimated at sixty to one hundred Asians each day.

Legend has it that Cleopatra consulted her physician about easy ways to die, chose the cobra's bite because it was believed to be both quick and painless. Actually, one bite by a five-foot specimen is likely to deliver sufficient venom to kill eight or more men.

An elephant, biggest of land animals, is not likely to survive more than three hours after a single injection from the cobra's hypodermic needle. Certain kraits produce venoms that are fifty times as toxic as potassium cyanide; no substance manufactured by nature is more awe-inspiring than death-dealing secretions from glands of reptiles.

Actually a kind of modified saliva, venom not only aids a

snake in its capture of quarry; it also helps in digestion—starting its cell-breaking work even before a victim is swallowed. Long recognized as elaborate proteins, venoms have been studied intensively for more than a century. More than 6000 technical papers have been published by researchers. Yet it is doubtful that science knows the exact composition and work of even one kind of venom.

Rattlesnakes and their kin have predominantly hemotoxic venoms—which damage blood cells and vessels, cause local congestion and bleeding. Cobras and coral snakes have predominantly neurotoxic venoms that affect heart, lungs, and nerve systems. No variety of venom is pure in type. Instead, all kinds include some elements that affect the blood and other factors that affect the nervous system.

Minute quantities of venom produce antibodies without leading to death, so the Pasteur Institute has devised ways to secure snake-bite serum from injected horses.

Specialists recognize that success in this endeavor represents only a first step across the threshold of mystery, however. For no one has a reasonable explanation for the way in which reaction to venom varies among creatures. Ounce for ounce, white mice are ten to twelve times as resistant as pigeons. Rattlesnakes can be killed by their own poison—but cobras are immune to injury by venom from their kind. This immunity is not universal, however; a king cobra bitten by a water moccasin died in twelve hours.

New medical uses for venom grow out of two factors. There is no absolute line of distinction between drugs and poisons. And fractional elements from complex organic poisons may show highly specialized effects.

All snake venoms are elaborate mixtures and compounds of protein fractions. Most are tasteless; that of the cobra is intensely bitter. Venom preserves its potency indefinitely even when dried, in which state it dissolves readily in both water and alcohol.

Cobra venom includes elements that cause blood platelets and cells to cluster, then disintegrate to release great quantities of histamine. Recent experiments indicate that a catalytic effect is involved; white blood cells seem to be used as agents in the destruction of red ones. Red cells are unharmed when the concentration of white ones falls below a critical level. So far, this reaction has not proved a useful tool for physicians.

Nerve-affecting fractions are unlocking long-closed doors of healing, however. In the case of cobra venoms, these toxins are concentrated in a special protein fraction that makes up one fifth the total protein in crude venom. Compounded largely of carbon, hydrogen, nitrogen, and sulphur, these elaborate substances have high molecular weights—ranging from 2500 to 4000 and above.

Dr. M. B. Greene, New York anesthetist, made medical history in 1938. That year he successfully used fractions from cobra venom to relieve pain from abdominal cancer. Until then, morphine was the only known treatment.

Subsequent use suggests that venom may eventually replace opiates in many uses. Morphine acts quickly, then rapidly combines with oxygen in the blood stream. Cobra venom acts more slowly but remains stable a great deal longer, permitting greater intervals between doses. Opiates are habit-forming and retard both vision and hearing. Venom is not habit-forming, actually increases acuteness of eyes and ears. In tapping tests for muscular reaction, morphine shows a retarding effect, while venom boosts the rate of response.

Venom-treated patients do not develop tolerance, so do not require the increase in dosage that is associated with opiates. Though venom relieves many types of pain fully as effectively as does morphine, side effects of the older drug are absent: patients show no eye changes, suffer no hallucinations.

Though use of venom is expanding rapidly, medical treatment by products of the Poison People is still in its infancy. Since Russell's viper kills by clotting the blood of victims, its venom is being tested for control of hemophilia. When venom is added to the blood stream in the ratio of one part to 100,000, blood of a "bleeder" clots in seventeen seconds—as opposed to thirty or forty minutes untreated.

Dentists have controlled severe bleeding from the tooth socket by packing with cobra venom. Rattlesnake venom is being tried in epilepsy. Drs. J. S. Chowan and R. N. Chopra have had "interesting results" treating nerve-type leprosy with cobra venom. It offers great promise for relief of symptoms associated with sciatica, shaking palsy, and inoperable cancer.

Where the future will lead, no one can predict. But at the mid-point of the twentieth century, this much is clear: the cobras and their cousins are fast regaining lead roles in the drama of medicine. For reasons quite different from those which prompted the reverence of ancient priests, tomorrow's scientists may pay tribute to crawling killers as revealers of secrets more profound than any whispered to Aesculapius by the centaur.

Storm Center of Medical Research

Dr. William W. Keen frowned, shook his head in bewilderment, and reread the letter.

"Archfiend," it began. "I hope your mother if she is living will die in the most terrible torture, and if she is dead that her soul will never know rest for having given life to such a vile monster as you . . ."

His attacker signed no name, but indicated that a dozen women were nightly praying for fulfillment of the writer's hope. It was expressed vigorously, bluntly, and without explanation.

None was needed. Dr. Keen had already received other letters, somewhat milder in tone, condemning him for an article published in the *Ladies' Home Journal.* Tempers were on edge in 1910, and the physician had dared to take a stand. Humanity, he said, has received tremendous benefits from medical research using the guinea pig and other laboratory animals.

Opponents of such experimentation were numerous, organized, and vocal. It is wrong, they insisted, to seek benefits for humans through processes that involve pain and sometimes death for animals. Experiments of one sort or another are as old as medicine. Extensive use of laboratory animals is a modern innovation, however.

Ancient physicians seem to have performed occasional operations on wild and domestic beasts. For the most part, the surgeon who wished to test a new technique looked about for human subjects. Criminals and slaves were frequently employed; so were captives taken in war.

Abandonment of these barbaric practices created a dilemma in medical circles. Before employing a new treatment upon his patients, any good doctor wants to know its probable effect. No matter how carefully refined, a novel theory needs to be tested. Though designed to relieve suffering and save lives, it may prove harmful or deadly. Only an actual test upon a living organism is likely to give clues to real understanding.

So pioneers of science began to experiment upon themselves. Throughout the eighteenth and nineteenth centuries, there were waves of daring and sometimes fatal tests.

Trying to learn the nature of the disease, in 1767 John Hunter deliberately infected himself with gonorrhea. A European physician almost died from an overdose of digitalis, taken in order to study its effects upon vision. In Boston, a Yankee doctor tested drugs by injecting them into his own veins. In Paris, a distinguished chemist swallowed strychnine before members of the French Academy of Sciences. He wished to show the action of charcoal in absorbing alkaloids; having guessed right, he survived.

A prominent Austrian was not so fortunate. Experimenting with effects of prussic acid, he killed himself. As late as 1906 the same fate met Fritz Schaudinn after he used his own body to study effects of an amoeba that thrives in the intestinal tract. James Simpson almost killed himself in trying to determine the best way to use chloroform. Pasteur contemplated injecting himself with rabies in order to test his serum. Pierre Curie actually bandaged radium bromide on his own arm so he could determine the severity of skin burns produced by the potent stuff.

So long as it was pursued in such fashion, medical research was slow, haphazard, and dangerous. During the nineteenth century, a number of discoveries contributed to radical changes in procedure.

First in point of time, and high in importance, was the discovery of anesthetics. There had already been considerable interest in using animals rather than men to study physiology and test surgical procedures. William Harvey had actually discovered circulation of the blood by dissecting living creatures. Most such experiments were futile, however. Subjects struggled so violently that it was impossible to perfect methods or measure results.

Use of anesthetics made it possible to operate upon relaxed subjects; development of antiseptics cut the mortality rate. So long as a heavy per cent of experiments ended in death from infection, no satisfactory results were possible. Research entered a new era when it became standard to make experiments under sterile conditions.

Still another group of advances were in the field of instrument design and manufacture. One of the most important new mechanical devices was the microscope—which surged into general use after 1850. Half a century later, the X ray once more extended the scope of research.

Fourth on the list of major changes was the development of antitoxins. Many harmful or "toxic" organisms were discovered through the radical new concept of bacteria as agents in disease. Some of these bacteria, it was learned, stimulate elaborate changes in the blood. A person who survives an illness may actually have in his veins an antitoxin—an agent which fights a particular toxin or bacteria. Incredibly, some antitoxins produced in bodies of animals can be used to ward off disease organisms which attack humans.

Given vital new incentives plus fresh tools with which to work, scientists were ready to launch medical research on a large scale. Now their chief need was a suitable subject for laboratory experiments. It had to be a living creature of low cost, easy to rear and handle, and resembling man in as many qualities as possible.

There was no sudden, dramatic solution. Rather, there was a long series of quiet, independent discoveries. Singly at first and later in groups of growing size, research workers turned to the guinea pig as an ideal animal for laboratory work.

This little rodent became known to Europeans only four centuries ago. Spanish adventurers found it in the Andes Mountains of South America. Natives of Peru and Bolivia had brought it under domestication in the ancient past. They had only three meat animals—the llama, alpaca, and cavy. Historians consider the latter to have been most numerous and important.

Early writers showed considerable interest in the animal. They noted that it has short legs of almost equal length, and that the tail is brief or rudimentary. It is somewhat strange, remarked some of them, that the little creature should have four toes on its front feet and only three on its rear ones. Though they knew the native name, most Spanish writers felt that *cavy* would mean nothing to their readers. So they called the animal *conejo,* or "rabbit."

Specimens were probably taken to Europe within a few decades after the time of Columbus. They attracted little interest in Spain and Italy. Then Dutch traders found a market for them in England. Perhaps because so many oddities came from Guinea, the strange animal which resembled a suckling pig came to be called the "guinea" pig.

Islanders first bought the little New World creatures as curiosities. Soon, however, they proved just right for rearing as household pets. Able to thrive on almost any vegetable diet, they cost little or nothing if a family cultivates a kitchen garden. They are easy to keep, clean, and gentle. In 1713, Richard Steele noted in his famous *Guardian* that the guinea pig of any great lady was likely to compete with poodles for a place on the lap of its mistress. Only in Germany was there extensive use of the little rodent as a table delicacy.

At least as early as 1806, an American pioneer was using the guinea pig in medical research. French, German, and English scientists gradually became interested in it.

In many respects, it proved the ideal subject for experiment. Since it is clean almost to the point of daintiness, the guinea pig is pleasant to handle. It is less subject to disease than rabbits—but can be infected with many maladies that plague humans. It is so gentle that an early *Natural History,* published in 1774, described it as "most timid of all quadrupeds." Adaptable to a wide range of foods and among the most prolific of domestic animals, its cost is far below that of most laboratory animals.

Hence, in Europe and America, guinea pigs came into great demand. Some scientific institutions reared their own. Most bought them from breeders, who realized about 50 per cent profit when animals sold for a dollar each. At no period was research pegged to the guinea pig alone. Yet it was used so widely and extensively that its name came to stand for an experimental creature of any kind.

World interest was aroused by dramatic discoveries involving "guinea pigs" of one type or another. Robert Koch's laboratories in Berlin competed with the Pasteur Institute in Paris for first place in number and importance of experiments. Everywhere, however, eager scientists cut open animals to study blood vessels, nerves, and organs. Every conceivable operation was tried, often in series involving hordes of guinea pigs and other subjects. How many hundreds of thousands of animals died as martyrs to medical progress no one knows.

Inevitably there was a wave of reaction. Some persons merely protested what they considered to be undue cruelty. Others insisted that research should not be pursued if it involves any pain whatever. Extremists, always in the minority but often supported by large numbers of followers, cried out for legislation prohibiting any kind of experiments which involve animals.

There is no doubt that guinea pigs, cats, dogs, horses, and other creatures actually suffered during operations when anesthetics were not used. It is equally clear that a few research workers must have been callous if not actually brutal. But on the whole, medical leaders were eager for humane treatment. British societies set up standards for treatment of animals in 1870–71.

Still, opponents of experiment were active and vocal. As a result of their activities, Parliament studied the problem. An elaborate set of laws, enacted in 1876, tried to take a middle ground between prohibition of research and research with controls.

Strangely, the British act—which is still in force—set up grades of privilege among animals. Horses, asses, and mules rate the highest rank; they may not be used for any experiment that can be performed upon an animal of any other species. Cats and dogs make up the second grade. Monkeys, rodents, and all other vertebrates form the third. Invertebrates are given no protection whatever!

Instead of leading to peace, British legislation seemed to fan the fires of controversy. Organizations were formed for the abolition of experiment—and were countered by leagues for the defense of research. In a period when medical laboratories had not yet begun to receive large grants, opponents of animal experiments contributed at least $500,000 to fight the scientists.

Inevitably, Charles Darwin was drawn into the fray. Though outspoken in endorsing humane methods, he stated that "physiology can progress only by the aid of experiments on living animals." Especially in England and the United States, medical societies launched elaborate educational programs.

Tension reached a peak in the decade prior to World War I. Dr. Keen was only one of many scientists who received anonymous letters and telephone calls, threats, and attacks by the press. Gross misrepresentations and actual fake exhibits were widely publicized. Research workers were accused of operating without anesthetics for the joy of giving pain. Powerful interests, including big newspaper chains, pressed for federal legislation to curb U.S. research. Numerous state and local restrictions were actually passed.

Most observers feel that the long-drawn fight is now nearly over. Scientists take every precaution to reduce or eliminate pain to the animals on which they experiment. Even the most confirmed of animal lovers are forced to recognize the dramatic results of research. So a national survey by the University of Chicago, made in 1949, found 85 per cent of Americans endorsing the use of laboratory animals.

Though it has won a permanent place in speech as a symbol for any subject of research, the guinea pig is now supplemented by many other creatures. White rats, fruit flies, dogs, and cats are probably the most numerous and important contributors to discovery. Research involving these creatures is divided into several major streams.

Surgical experiments held the spotlight until 1875. Great numbers of animals were cut for the study of their glands, organs, circulatory and nervous systems. Practically all operations that are now routine were first performed on guinea pigs and cats. Whenever a pioneer developed a new tool or technique, he tested it in the laboratory before introducing it into the hospital.

Today only one experiment in twenty involves surgery. This does not mean that scientists have stopped pushing back the frontiers of knowledge about physiology. Rather, the dramatic opening of new fields has multiplied the non-surgical use of animals.

Louis Pasteur kicked off an exciting quest for ways to develop serums and antitoxins. French farmers were losing their sheep, whole flocks at a time, from outbreaks of anthrax. Pasteur showed that bacteria cause the disease—and in 1881 developed a preventive inoculation. His serum was made from body fluids of animals. A century earlier, Jenner had found a way to vaccinate humans against cowpox (our modern smallpox). But until the germ theory of disease was formulated, no one knew why vaccines were effective.

Following the lead of Pasteur, scientists launched an international race to find serums. Using guinea pigs as hosts for the malady, a Brazilian doctor tried to perfect a vaccine for yellow fever. German and Japanese research workers pooled their findings, in 1890 discovered the antitoxin treatment for diphtheria. In the decade after public immunization was launched in England, the death rate was cut to one fourth its centuries-old level.

Sir T. Lauder Brunton determined to master snake venoms,

for he knew that in India alone the reptiles claimed 30,000 human victims a year. Using guinea pigs for much of his work, the British scientist developed an antidote—not uniformly effective, but giving medicine a major boost.

Pasteur himself passed microbes through monkeys and other host animals, prepared a serum for treatment of rabies. Tetanus was licked by use of body fluids from infected horses. Horses are still standard as living incubators for tetanus antitoxin and toxoid, antivenom serum, diphtheria antitoxin and toxoid, plus a toxoid for gangrene resulting from poison gas. One animal can produce each year enough serum to protect 75,000 persons from tetanus.

At the Rockefeller Institute, two specialists developed a serum for use against spinal meningitis. Their findings grew out of experiments which involved about a hundred guinea pigs and some two dozen monkeys.

While these spectacular results were being achieved, other scientists were busy investigating effects of drugs and food substances. Such complex and dangerous compounds as morphine, digitalis, belladonna, and cocaine were gradually mastered. One after another, vitamins and food poisons were isolated and studied. Since guinea pigs have blood that closely resembles our own, the docile rodents have been central in many discoveries. They are used to test effects of liver extracts, antibiotics, synthetic vitamins—and even sex hormone creams.

Before the turn of the last century, medical leaders recognized that complex substances can't be judged by chemical analysis alone. In order to test their nature or strength, it is necessary to use a living organism.

In London, workers at the Lister Institute learned how to use guinea pigs to test the city's milk supply for tuberculosis infection. Diphtheria antitoxin was standardized on the little

South American animal. Many new and virulent strains of disease organisms, and drugs to fight them, have been mastered through use of guinea pigs and rabbits. Insulin to combat diabetes was first standardized on rabbits, while the heart stimulant, digitalis, is still tested upon cats.

Practically all major medical developments since 1875 have involved experiments or tests on animals. White mice were used to find the effects of penicillin and tyrothricin. Cats were the first creatures to be placed in an iron lung. Guinea pigs provided results which led to a radical new concept of heredity: various traits of mammals are believed to be inherited independently. At Notre Dame, J. A. Reyniers recently reared guinea pigs under completely sterile conditions. For the first time in history, it became possible to study effects of bacteria upon animals which have been sheltered from birth.

In spite of the increasing use of other organisms, the guinea pig retains a kind of immortality. To assess its contributions to mankind is impossible, for they have been indirect as well as direct. As the focal point of the once-vital controversy over methods of medical research, the New World rodent symbolizes all experimental animals. So long as laboratory investigations continue, animals will probably figure in them. Taking the long look, it is just possible that the guinea pig has affected human destiny fully as much as any other creature, wild or domestic.

Leptinotarsa decemlineata: The Bug That Changed Its Mind

Ex-president Truman shares a doubtful honor with General MacArthur and Dean Acheson. In all the by-ways of natural history, they are the only three world leaders whose faces have been portrayed on the heads of *Leptinotarsa decemlineata.*

Of course, that cumbersome name was not used by cartoonists of the East German government. When they issued a propaganda leaflet in 1950, they called it "Potato Bugs under Magnifying Glass." Striped beetles shown in the sketch had the features of the three U.S. leaders.

Though it is now comical, in the critical years following the war's end, the matter had all the ingredients of an international incident. For the leaflet charged that U.S. planes were flying over eastern Germany, Poland, and other satellite countries. Airmen were said to be dropping, not explosives, but biological bombs—in the form of Colorado potato beetles.

Pravda quoted an agricultural official as saying that 273,

838 of the little gluttons had been found in Saxony and Thuringia, 103,758 in Mecklenburg.

Potatogrowers behind the Iron Curtain muttered threats, testified that the beetles were dropped on May 22. Soviet diplomats delivered a formal note of protest to the U.S. Ambassador in Moscow.

Official replies were sent from the U. S. Department of State to representatives of both Russia and Czechoslovakia. One document labeled the charge as "ridiculous." Another said "The Embassy ventures to suggest the inherent unsuitability of the potato bug as an instrument of national policy."

Actually, the idea was neither new nor altogether fantastic. According to Science Service, U.S. entomologists seriously suggested dropping beetles into German potato fields near the close of World War I. And when the greedy insects threatened to gain a foothold on Britain in 1940, the *Illustrated London News* speculated that they might have been "deliberately introduced by the enemy."

Few insects are more suited for use in biological warfare; none matches the speed with which the American beetle has swept from obscurity to international prominence.

As recently as a century and a half ago, the insect was unknown to scientists. Thomas Say, sometimes called the "father of American entomology," collected specimens in Missouri and Arkansas about 1823.

Say was struck by the brilliant yellow and black stripes which run along its wing covers. So he coined the name *decemlineata*—or "ten lines"—to describe it. Forty years later, taxonomists placed the species in the genus *Leptinotarsa*—or "slender-footed."

For three decades after its discovery, the slender-footed beetle with ten stripes remained in the category of a rare, even an exotic, specimen. Its range was limited to the eastern slopes of the Rocky Mountains. Numbers were small, for it fed only upon plants of the nightshade family: the sandbur, buffalo bur, or beaked nightshade.

Almost exactly a century ago, the beetle changed its diet. Settlers had begun pushing into its region. Occasionally a farmer or his wife scratched a few shallow furrows in the ground and planted Irish potatoes. This vine, itself a relative of nightshade plants, was investigated by the gay native beetle.

How the insect was attracted to the potato no one knows. No mystery of nature is deeper or more complex than that which shrouds the eating habits of wild creatures. Many species of animals and insects live on one kind of plant food, choosing it in preference to related types. Somehow, the tiny leaf-eating beetle discovered that potato metabolism is precisely geared to its own. Leaves of the cultivated plant contain just the right ingredients, suitably arranged.

So there was a mass desertion of wild nightshades in favor of tender, wholesome potatoes—which settlers thoughtfully planted in convenient patches.

This epochal event took place shortly before 1859. It was not mentioned in newspapers of the period, and contemporary historians took no notice. Soon, however, financial consequences loomed much larger than the total cost of the Civil War.

Attack of the beetles upon man's biggest food crop coincided almost exactly with the beginning of bloodshed between Union and Confederate forces. Yet even battles couldn't keep the striped invader in obscurity. In the Colorado region it became so destructive that settlers gave it the popular name which has since been adopted in many parts of the world. By 1865 it had swept eastward as far as Illinois.

Benjamin Walsh, state entomologist, described its spread as similar to the march of an invading army.

Moving east at more than fifty miles a year, the tide of insects engulfed the whole Middle West by 1870. Ohio was reached and conquered. In 1871, C. V. Riley described a vast horde of beetles. Temporarily halted on the shores of Lake Erie, "they took to ships, chips, staves, any floating object which presented itself," and moved ahead.

Wave after wave poured forward—to Ontario, New Brunswick, Manitoba, and Nova Scotia in the north. South to Louisiana, Alabama, Mississippi. East to West Virginia, Delaware, Connecticut, North Carolina.

Advance contingents reached the Atlantic coast in 1874; nothing but mopping-up action remained in the main area of invasion. In just sixteen years, a curious museum specimen had become a major threat to U.S. food supplies. It was firmly established throughout an area of more than 500,000,000 acres.

Unless beetles are checked, they may eat every scrap of leaf from each plant in a potato patch. Though they rarely do direct damage to tubers, losses range up to 100 per cent of the crop. Desperate U.S. planters sent their families into fields to hand-pick vines. This was effective, but too slow for wide use. Several kinds of brushes were invented, with which insects were swept from leaves into pans of water or oil. Still the annual potato yield crept downward.

Then someone stumbled upon a radical new approach to the problem.

Householders of the period took great pride in adorning their homes with fashionable green shutters. Paint manufacturers had tried many formulas, found only one of them satisfactory. So practically all shutter paint was compounded from Paris green—a bright powder resulting from combination of arsenic with acetate of copper.

Legend has it that a Missouri farmer, perhaps just home from the Civil War, had a little paint left over after putting a coat of it on his shutters. So he tossed the remainder into a clump of vines badly infested with the Colorado potato bug. Next day he noticed that hundreds of them lay on their backs, dead.

Whether or not that is the exact manner of the discovery, someone west of the Mississippi River did launch the use of Paris green as a weapon against insects. Many experiments were made. As a dust, it was mixed with flour, ashes, plaster, or slaked lime—for the pure chemical is injurious to foliage. Various formulas were devised for pouring and spraying it in liquid form. By 1874, Gray's Improved Sprinkler enabled an operator to carry a tank on his back. Manipulating short pieces of hose, he sprinkled the deadly liquid on two rows of plants at once.

Not only was this the first mechanical device for ridding plants of insects; the beetle killer was the first of formal insecticides. Its adoption launched a new era in global ecology—man's use of chemicals to eliminate or reduce populations of undesirable insects. Many experts were jubilant. They predicted a brave new world, in which the potato bug and all other such pests would be mastered.

Such unbounded enthusiasm was soon found to rest upon a shallow foundation. Development of scientific insecticides did mark a major forward step on the part of mankind. But chemical warfare against tiny enemies is far from simple and may never be decisive. Most or all forms of life exert tremendous expansive pressure. Natural biological processes tend to reduce or overcome the effects of death-dealing forces.

The reproductive power of the Colorado beetle soon

proved more potent than Paris green. This insect lays its yellowish eggs in bunches of thirty or forty. About one sixteenth of an inch long, they are glued to the under side of potato leaves. A typical female lays some 600 or more eggs during a period of a month. Some are much more prolific; one count in 1914 showed 1879 eggs from a single beetle.

Within a week after an egg is laid, it holds a fully developed larva. With the aid of hatching spines formed on the thorax, the grub cuts its way out of the shell. It begins to feed on potato leaves at once. Growth is so rapid that there are four successive molts in the two or three weeks required to reach full size.

Now fat from feasting, the larva takes leave of its host plant. Descending into the soil, it makes a spherical cell and enters a five to ten day pupal stage. Emerging from it as an adult beetle, it promptly climbs to the nearest potato vine and starts eating again. Within a few days it is ready to begin its own orgy of egg placing.

Where summers are long, it is possible for the Colorado beetle to go through three generations in one season. Theoretically, the total brood of a single insect may soar past the million mark within three months after she crawls from her mother's egg. Insecticides and natural enemies keep the actual number much lower. Remove their effects, however, and beetles could render the potato useless for agriculture.

Long ago, weary farmers termed their foe the 'rithmetic bug. For, said they, it adds to misery, subtracts from the harvest, divides attention—and multiplies like the dickens.

Aside from its fecundity, the insect poses a constant threat because of its ability to adapt to widely varying sets of conditions. There is probably no truth to the story that striped scouts have been caught inspecting the records of wholesalers, to see what planters have ordered seed potatoes for next spring. But since it passes its winters hibernating deep in the soil, the beetle from Colorado does flourish even in cold regions. In just fifty years, it pressed from Alberta to outposts 400 miles nearer the Arctic Circle.

Since it is not a strong flier, early observers predicted that the beetle would be stopped by major rivers. They were easily crossed, however. Swarms of insects, usually reluctant to stop eating, frequently abandon their birthplace during storms. Spreading delicate rose-tinted wings, they rise into the wind and may glide for miles—often into territory not previously invaded by their kind.

"One thing will stop 'em," gloated European farmers. "They'll never get across the Atlantic."

Scientists disagreed. They pointed out that the adult beetle goes through a drying and hardening process as cold weather approaches. Fortified for sub-zero temperatures, it can survive under extremely difficult circumstances.

Entomologists launched a campaign to arouse the people of England, France, and Germany. They warned that beetles could easily stow away on ships—either in bags of potatoes or as chance passengers—and reach new shores.

Great excitement followed when a few were discovered in Belgium in 1877. Though they were quickly eradicated, English leaders predicted that new waves would follow. They warned that economic disaster, and even famine, could result if the insect were to become established in Britain. Posters were placed on porches of rural churches throughout England and Ireland. A formal bill for control of the greedy immigrant was introduced into Parliament by the Duke of Richmond.

Many persons snickered at taking a bug so seriously. Several prominent European journalists wrote editorials questioning whether the American insect would survive even if introduced. A London manufacturer brought out a novelty line of studs, pinheads, and fancy stationery—all featuring the much-talked-of insect.

Danger to Europe was minimized by a prominent U.S. scientist. He discounted the threat, not because he doubted the possibility of an invasion, but because insecticides were proving so potent. "The American cultivator," he said, "by means of intelligence and a little Paris green, is pretty much master." Editors of England's famous *Spectator* magazine took an even more optimistic view. They described the early spray apparatus as "rather comic," expressed the hope that England's farm workers would never be seen scattering chemicals in the fields.

Several times in the succeeding half century, Colorado beetles were found in Britain or on the Continent. In each case, quick action led to eradication.

It was a different story in 1922.

That year, hordes of the gaudy insects were found in fields stretching for miles through the department of Gironde, France. They probably accompanied U.S. troops during World War I—so became well entrenched during and immediately after the fighting.

England and Germany declared a state of quarantine. Belgium equipped troops with flame throwers, stationed guards along her borders. It was too late. One international boundary after another was passed: Belgium, Holland, Switzerland, Germany, Poland, Czechoslovakia, Russia, the Balkan states. . . .

By 1948, many Russians were using matches from boxes which showed a beetle above the caption: "Proclaim the harm of the Colorado potato beetle and warn farmers." Next year there was a nationwide conference of Polish officials to discuss countermeasures against the insect. Crops were threatened in both East Germany and parts of Russia.

U.S. diplomats declare that Soviet charges of bug dropping were intended to cover up for communist failure in stemming the tide of six-legged invaders. So far, British efforts have been more successful. Any citizen who finds what he thinks may be a potato eater is required to send it to the Ministry of Agriculture. If identified as a Colorado beetle, a "flying squad" is dispatched from the ministry's Plant Protection, Ltd. Plants are hand-picked, then treated with poison. Even the ground is sprayed. Such tactics have prevented the establishment of permanent colonies.

They may be set up in Britain any year, however. In 1950, so many were blown from France that school children were sent to comb beaches of the Channel Islands. Three years earlier, a single season was marked by discovery of fifty-seven small groups—chiefly in southern England. Relentlessly spreading to new regions, it is likely that the hungry Colorado beetle will eventually feast wherever potatoes are grown.

Yet the victory of biology over chemistry is far from complete. Curiously, it was the potato eater who touched off investigations which produced man's most potent new weapons against insects.

Paul Mueller, chemist of Basle, Switzerland, was among those who became alarmed about the establishment of the Colorado beetle in Europe. He recognized that the insect could never be conquered by use of then-standard arsenicals. So he set out to get a more toxic substance. He found it in the long-obscure compound now world-famous as DDT.

Mueller quickly saw that DDT has implications far beyond control of the potato beetle. He experimented upon houseflies and other insects, released his findings just in time to permit Allied forces to take advantage of them. Use of DDT suppressed typhus and other insect-borne diseases, reduced the death toll in the wake of war. As a result, the Swiss—who is not a physician—received the 1948 Nobel Prize in medicine.

Use of DDT and related compounds has greatly thinned the ranks of the Colorado beetle and other insect foes. Hence per-acre potato yield has jumped nearly 50 per cent since 1946.

Long an international problem, the potato bug has been investigated by an unofficial European committee since 1936. In 1947, an official International Committee on Colorado Beetle Control was set up with headquarters in Paris. Hundreds of research projects are in progress throughout the Western world.

How long man can maintain a healthy margin of advantage is anyone's guess. Hope of exterminating the winged marauder is all but nil. About the best that science can do is to keep it in check by constant use of insecticides, plus a stream of improvements in every phase of potato culture.

Though all previous efforts have failed, the best hope for lasting victory lies in changing the nature of the potato itself. If leaves can be made unpalatable or toxic to the insect, without affecting the nature of the tubers, the potato of the future will be safe from its chief foe.

Though such developments sound easy in theory, they are most difficult in practice. For no one yet knows why the obscure little feeder on sandburs changed its mind and switched to potatoes. Experts are acquainted with four close relatives of the beetle; all of them feed on wild plants of the order which includes the potato. Yet none of them has taken a liking to the cultivated plant.

Colorado beetles can eat many different plants in emergency. They have been seen feeding on such varied species as the tomato, eggplant, thorn apple, horse nettle, cabbage, thistle, petunia, Jimson weed—even tobacco and pepper. Not one of these plants affords the insect a balanced diet. Some of them sustain its life, but it thrives and multiplies only on a one-item menu: fresh leaves of the Irish potato. Unless it loses its appetite or people quit planting potatoes, it is apparently here to stay.

The Rat: Strange By-Product of Civilization

Measured by almost any standard, the rat is the most important four-legged foe of modern man. A twelve-ounce engine of destruction with built-in features that make him a specialist in transmitting disease, the rodent easily surpasses all other animal pests in number, cost, and menace.

It is a minor whimsy of Mother Nature that this scourge of nations has soared to prominence as a result of human impact on global life zones.

Rare and scattered clues suggest that rats have been around for many thousands of years. Bones have even been found in association with relics from men of the Stone Age. Yet the cutting animal has had a very brief career as a villain. It has played such a role for less than a thousand years—a mere instant of biological time.

Literature of classical Greece and Rome abounds in references to animals, large and small. There are several allusions to mice, but not so much as a single word about rats. This factor, plus the absence of their bones from excavated sites, indicates they were rare if not altogether missing from ancient cities. Not until late in the twelfth century A.D. did any writer make a clear reference to the rodent.

Theory has it that wild rats of the Arabian deserts found they could fare better in villages than among sand dunes. So they moved to town and became dependent on mankind and gradually spread into more densely settled regions. If this view is correct, they were numerous but not especially important by the time of the Crusades. When Christian warriors returned to Europe, African rats stowed away on their ships and soon established outposts in the new land.

Slaty black in color, the rat is now known to zoologists as *Rattus rattus*. A skilled and graceful climber, it easily runs along pipes, wires, and ropes. Its tail—which is slightly longer than its body—serves as a balance so effective that it can jump from one perch to another almost as nimbly as a squirrel.

Efforts at control were sporadic and ineffective. In some cities, various kinds of bounty were offered. For instance, Jews of fifteenth-century Frankfurt, Germany, received special privileges in return for annual tribute in the form of 5000 rat tails. Professional ratcatchers became so numerous that they were organized into guilds; in Shakespeare's time, such a fellow sometimes enjoyed considerable honor in his town.

In spite of attacks by professionals and amateurs, the black rat had a field day. Europe was literally overrun. Damage to food and other commodities shot upward at a really alarming rate. People grumbled, tried new traps and poisons, passed laws.

They did not recognize that its role as a vandal is the smallest part of the rat's menace. Only in recent centuries has it become clear that epidemics of typhus and bubonic plague were linked with the invasion of Europe by the rodent.

Though it must have existed much earlier, plague did not

become epidemic until modern times. In the five or six generations before Columbus' voyage, more than 34,000,000 persons died of it. Europe's population was reduced by one fourth. Spanish armies in Granada lost six men from plague to every man felled by arrows of the Moors. Transmitted to man by fleas from rats, plague hit London in 1665. Before it subsided, there were 100,000 casualties.

Many persons regard the rat-borne disease as "medieval," of historical interest only. It is true that there have been no major epidemics in the Western Hemisphere in nearly three centuries. Health authorities have checked it quickly in each U.S. outbreak: San Francisco, 1907; New Orleans, 1914; Galveston, 1920.

Lacking money and equipment, doctors of India have not matched that record. In the quarter century after 1898, plague killed as many natives of India as there are people in Chicago, Philadelphia, Atlanta, Dallas, Miami, and Los Angeles combined.

And that's only one facet of the story.

Through the agency of the lice whom they harbor, rats also serve to transmit typhus. Even plague and cholera have not rolled up a more impressive record of death. Epidemic for only four centuries, typhus has claimed at least 200,000,000 victims. Historians generally write the records of nations in terms of kings and generals. Hans Zinsser has pointed out, in his famous book on *Rats, Lice, and History,* that rat-spread typhus influenced Western civilization far more than any great man whose name appears in all the schoolbooks.

It would be sheer guesswork to estimate the total impact of rat-linked disease and death. Black rats of the past and brown ones of the present rank so high among global killers that most authorities are content with a general statement. In less than ten centuries, agree experts, diseases involving rats as agents have taken more human lives than all the wars and revolutions ever fought.

Plague and typhus do not exhaust the list. A rat is a living freighter whose design is just right for transporting a cargo of bacteria. He can digest almost anything, so after a meal in the garbage dump may slip into a building for dessert: random samplings from exposed food. With feet still wet from a jaunt through his favorite sewer, he may prowl casually over the stock of the corner grocery. His blood stream and stomach harbor disease-producing organisms ranging from those of amoebic dysentery and infectious jaundice to rabies and tularemia.

So far, all attempts to exterminate the rat have failed miserably. Hundreds of inventors have perfected traps—but none are more than moderately effective. Dogs, cats, ferrets, and even weasels are still used to hunt them—but seldom do more than thin the ranks temporarily.

Long-used natural poisons have about seen their day. Powerful new synthetic compounds of several types have been used with considerable success. One of them, 1080, is so deadly to humans and livestock that only experts are permitted to use it. Another, ANTU, is fatal to brown rats but comparatively harmless to many other mammals. Warfarin, most publicized of new poisons, prevents blood from clotting and causes rats to die from internal bleeding.

A few optimists have predicted that these and other chemical weapons can reduce the rat to negligible importance. Others consider such a view to be wishful thinking. In the known history of rats, they point out, there has been only one instance of a really decisive victory.

It was won, not by men, but by rats.

History's strangest conquest is believed to have been launched shortly before 1727. In that year, hordes of odd brown rats were seen scurrying through Russia. When they came to the Volga, the stream of migrants plunged into the river. Thousands drowned, but great numbers crossed to the western bank.

Some authorities think this fierce rodent came from Chinese Mongolia. Others believed its original home was somewhere near the Caspian Sea. At any rate, it was unknown in Europe before the eighteenth century.

Once it penetrated new regions, however, its advance was sure and rapid. A few specimens reached England in 1728. Popular belief linked the brown marauder with timber ships from Norway. Hence it is now almost universally known as the Norway rat—*Rattus norvegicus.*

Short-tailed and blunt-nosed by comparison with the black rat, the evil-eyed newcomer proved much more fierce. Attacking its well-established cousin, the brown rat won a series of smashing victories. Blacks are still dominant in South America, where the climate gives them an advantage. Almost everywhere else except in seaports, browns have exterminated their slender foes. This development in the rat world has no biological parallel except those wars of conquest in which humans of one kind have all but wiped out humans of other kinds.

Brown invaders reached North America some time just before or after the Revolution. They spread up and down the Atlantic seaboard within a decade. When miners made their epic dash to California, rats went with them. Working inland from both coasts, they were soon established throughout temperate North America.

Meanwhile, other evil-eyed pioneers moved from Europe toward the East. They set up successful colonies wherever they stopped. Hence they are now firmly entrenched in regions that make up about half the world's land surface. At the mid-point of the twentieth century, no other mammal except man holds an equal territory. Brown rats of the world probably outnumber their hosts; if so, they are the most numerous animals on earth.

Willingness to eat just about anything has been a major factor in the rat's world conquest. Adults eat about fifty pounds of food a year. Their menu: almost anything they can cut. They've been known to gorge on paint, shoe leather, soap, and rubber insulation from electric wires. Enterprising colonies have cut into the bellies of swine, dug turnips from the ground, and even feasted on oil-rich toenails of sleeping elephants.

No one knows how many rats there are in the world. In the United States alone there are thought to be some 175,000,000 —give or take a few millions.

This estimate rests on data from many campaigns against the prowling guest at man's tables. In Baltimore, one year of activity by civic forces led to some 46,000 casualties among the city's rats. U. S. Department of Agriculture workers killed 7,500,000 in a single big three-state operation. In order to do so they had to use 400,000 traps, carloads of poisoned grain, and about 1,000,000 pounds of little sausages well laced with poison.

According to the best guess of the U. S. Fish and Wildlife Service, direct rat damage in this country ranges somewhere near $200,000,000 a year. World totals soar far into the billions—precisely how far there is no way to determine.

Actual eating by rats is perhaps the smallest part of their drain on civilization. They destroy many times as much as they cram into their bellies. It is generally believed that their toll exceeds that of all other animal pests combined.

Part of this wholesale destruction rests on a biological base.

Incisor teeth of the rat appear eight or ten days after birth. Both lowers and uppers are "rootless," or permanently growing. Throughout life, the incisors advance at the rate of about four inches a year. If one is lost from the rat's upper jaw or knocked out of line so that it ceases to meet its opposite below, the bottom one may push up so high it pierces the brain cavity and causes death.

Total growth of upper and lower cutting teeth in the normal rat's three-year life amounts to about 29.5 inches. Obviously, if the rodent didn't work constantly at the job of wearing down his teeth, they'd soon become so long he'd go around with his mouth permanently propped open.

This factor may account, at least in part, for persistent lifelong gnawing and chewing. Observation suggests that the typical individual uses his teeth at least half his waking hours. When he isn't actually eating, he's ripping and cutting—sometimes, it seems, almost as though for sheer fun.

Given a few hours in a warehouse, a single rat may tear holes in dozens of sacks—flour, grain, feed, coffee, or even fertilizer. Instead of dining on two whole potatoes or apples, a hungry fellow is likely to take random bites from a score of them. Apparently killing for the joy of it, rats have slaughtered as many as 1500 baby chicks, 325 broilers in a single foray.

The cutting edges of their teeth are extremely hard. For no known reason except a remote possibility that water may be their objective, rats sometimes gnaw through lead pipes. Laboratory albinos—weaklings by comparison with wild cousins—cut through two inches of Foamglass in an eight-night test. Two nights less were required to gnaw a hole in an aluminum sheet a full half inch thick. Wild rats have been known to cut through four inches of solid concrete floor. They've gnawed holes in dams and started floods, and once threw much of New York into darkness by stripping insulation from wires in such fashion that a major generating system was short-circuited.

Though ordinary ones are not so adept as the notorious pack rat, they do steal small objects and carry them to the nest. Digging into dens under a tenement, exterminators have found such trinkets as keys, coins, a belt buckle, lipstick tube, and shoehorn. Matches are often scattered through such piles of loot.

It is no myth, declare experts, that rats start fires both by cutting insulation from electric wires and by accidentally striking matches. Running to his nest with an ordinary friction match in his mouth, the rat drops it when it happens to strike. If it falls into a pile of litter, there may be another fire of undetermined origin.

Few if any individual rats ever start more than one blaze, however. That conclusion is based on the remarkable way they react to traps and poisons. A single experience often causes a rat to avoid a given source of danger for the rest of its life.

Dr. Curt P. Richter, of Johns Hopkins, devoted five years to a study of the rat's dietary choices. Given free access to separate containers of minerals, vitamins, carbohydrates, fats, and proteins, laboratory animals selected each in proportions making for good health. That, insist some analysts, is more than many humans will do.

Rats can dig their own burrows, but are smart enough to invade and take over the quarters of other creatures. They aren't fond of water, but swim when the situation demands it. Sailors long vowed that they know when a ship is in bad condition—so desert vessels about to sink. This belief lies behind the almost universal practice of calling any kind of deserter or traitor a "rat." Bizarre as it sounds, the notion may not be completely unfounded. In old wooden ships, rats were undoubtedly the first on board to know about new leaks—which may have prompted an exodus at the next port.

Many wild creatures languish in captivity, quickly die. Not the gray rat. He exercises voluntarily, quickly adapts to almost any condition in which life can be sustained. Making educational movies about them, producers found they soon ignored intense light. Camera noise was a bigger problem. It was solved by running nonsense sounds continuously at a high volume, masking all minor noises. Four-footed actors went about their business, oblivious of both sounds and lights.

Most exterminators agree that an old veteran, whom they call a "Moby Dick," can master almost any kind of trap. He kicks it around until it goes off, then calmly eats the bait—unless he whiffs poison in it.

One expert vows he's watched individual rats that like music so well they click their teeth in applause. That story, which hasn't won general acceptance by scientists, may rank with others which tell of young ones leading the old and blind to safety in time of danger. And there are those who vow they've seen rats steal food by dipping their tails into bottles too small to admit a snout.

Perhaps the most fantastic of rat stories is that which explains the way they steal eggs. Though some scoff at it, the tale has been current since the thirteenth century. According to it, rats organize when they wish to plunder a nest or crate. One grabs an egg in his forepaws and rolls over on his back; another catches his tail and drags him to their den. Whether that account is accurate or not, *somehow* rats do move eggs considerable distances and over obstacles. Eggs disappeared from one hatchery at the rate of eighty dozen a week. When humans made an assault on rat dens, many eggs were found stockpiled in underground storerooms of the gray thieves.

This much is absolutely clear: rats quickly beat every lethal device aimed at them. It is still too early to know whether new synthetic poisons will retain their effectiveness over a period of years. Rats may learn to recognize and avoid them. Albinos studied in the laboratory quickly learned to identify a magazine advertisement for ice cream—then select it from half a dozen assorted ads. They also have the capacity to select one letter of the alphabet from a row of mixed ones, or pick a given ink blot from a display of several.

Some psychologists assert that rats make better scores on five-way choices than on two-way ones. This, they think, is because any simple problem quickly bores a subject and he quits trying.

Intelligence alone would make the rat a worthy foe. In addition, he is fortified with a biological heritage that enables him to overcome almost any partial victory by two-legged opponents. Given ideal conditions, a single female can produce ten litters in a year—each with about ten young. Potentially, one pair can have 350,000,000 descendants in three years.

Such a rate of production is of course fantastic. Ecological zones aren't as simple as that. Yet the practical possibilities are vast enough. Given a city block in which rat population is reduced to two males and ten females, descendants can easily increase to 3000 within two years. Using every known weapon—including cyanide or other poison gas—professional exterminators seldom kill more than 95 per cent of the rats in a region. So it is only a matter of time before survivors bring the population back to old levels.

Extermination on the global or even national level is not a real possibility in the foreseeable future. Control is a different matter. It can probably be accomplished by three processes, no one of which may be omitted. First, use concrete and steel to rat-proof buildings. Second, eliminate open sources of food, such as garbage dumps and waste heaps. Third, wage a continuous war with traps and poisons.

As a lasting solution to the rat problem, periodic killing without other measures is about as effective as treating leprosy with calamine lotion.

Rats have multiplied at an astonishing rate in the past few centuries because man has created a special ecological niche which is tailor-made for them. Civilization gives the rat abundant food on an all-year basis—plus protection from natural foes.

Nature offers no rat cafeterias that approximate the bakery, poultry shop, stable, distillery, feed mill, warehouse, food store, wharf, slaughterhouse, sewer, garbage dump—or even a home where food is constantly on hand.

Nor does nature provide spacious shelters from which hereditary enemies are banished. Many creatures consider the rat a choice tidbit. It is hunted and eaten by most predatory mammals—including specialists like ferrets, weasels, and skunks. Neither householders nor businessmen encourage such rat killers to hang around. Nor is there a more hearty welcome for snakes, owls, storks, herons, eagles, or vultures.

In effect, man has built special rat havens which he calls cities and farms. He stocks them with abundant food which is on hand in wet weather or dry, hot or cold. These life zones are just right for one of the planet's distinctive organisms—hence it pushes into them and maintains the maximum population that is possible under the dynamics of the situation.

To overcome so well sheltered a pest, it would be necessary to make a major change in some aspect of the man-rat complex. To date, only one really effective idea has been suggested: man should put the rat on his menu as a delicacy. Failing this or an equally radical change, it appears likely that cousin rat will continue to be man's guest for a long time to come.

Curtain Call for the Buffalo

Yankee civilization served as a cultural bomb that blew one of the world's most magnificent animals into obscurity. Two million years in the shaping, incredibly vast herds of buffaloes were wiped out in less than one quarter of a century. For during the roaring years after the Civil War, cracks of breech-loading rifles and toots of steam locomotives punctuated the passing of a way of life for half the North American continent.

Until 1521, no white man had laid eyes on the animal.

Fighting their way into the capital city of the Aztecs, Hernando Cortés and his men found many marvels. Among them was a "Mexican bull" that formed a prize exhibit in the menagerie of King Montezuma. Conquistadores described the queer animal as having hair like a lion, a hump like a camel, and crooked shoulders. They regarded it as rare and exotic, not likely to be found anywhere in significant numbers.

Small wonder that they gaped at the beast. Three quarters of a ton of ferocity, the typical bull is about ten feet long and stands nearly six feet high at the shoulders. Body and hindquarters are peculiar in hue, difficult to describe. Audubon spoke of the bison's characteristic color as "between a dark umber and liver-shining brown." Bluish-purple tongue wagging above his ten-inch chin beard, the big fellow's head seems almost nightmarish—utterly unlike that of any familiar European creature.

Cabeza de Vaca saw several specimens of the "crooke-backed oxen" when he blazed a trail from Texas to West Mexico in 1536. Another dozen years passed before Coronado reached real buffalo country and discovered that the animal was much more than a queer species suitable for exhibition in zoological gardens.

For it was on the great western plains that the American bison flourished to a degree unmatched by any big animal of recent geological epochs. Even the antelopes and zebras of South Africa never became so numerous. Monarch of grasslands that spread from Canada to Texas, the buffalo achieved a population calculated to range somewhere near 60,000,000.

As late as the Civil War period, Charles Goodnight was awed by infrequent encounters with buffalo hordes. Writing of a southern herd—much smaller than some northern ones—he described it as about twenty-five miles wide and fifty miles long, "as thick as they could graze." Many contemporaries supported his report that when one rode upon such a herd, as far as one could see "the whole country was covered with what appeared to be a monstrous moving brown blanket."

Elaborate chains of circumstance, duplicated nowhere else in the world, made North America a haven for buffaloes. Some of the most stirring events in the planetary drama took place in the Pleistocene epoch.

During at least part of this geological period, America was linked with Asia. Hundreds of thousands of years ago, big-boned animals crossed northern land bridges and invaded the New World. Some species were hardy enough to hold their own against wolves, hairy enough to brave icy winters. This was the era when the woolly rhinoceros and the hairy mammoth flourished inside the Arctic Circle.

Among the animals that wandered to new regions were several types of fierce wild oxen. Some had horns that measured six feet across, could disembowel a timber wolf with a single slash. Dependent upon grass, they made annual migrations with the changing seasons. The limited extent of pasturage served to restrict their numbers.

During the global symphony that geologists know as earth's latest ice age, nature carved out a colossal region superbly adapted for grass eaters. Several times, glaciers grew to cover much of North America—then receded toward the Pole. There were accompanying cycles of mass movement on the part of both plants and animals. Now driven south, now pressing far to the north, some species perished while others were modified in body structure and habits.

During some of these periods, the woolly mammoth ranged as far south as New England. Musk oxen spread into Arkansas and Texas, while walruses swam along the coast of Georgia. When the pendulum swung back, now-tropical species such as the tapir and ground sloth flourished in Canada and Alaska.

Along with their fellows, ancient ox-like creatures underwent a series of changes. Those that became ancestors of the modern bison developed a broad skull, plus spines on their shoulder vertebrae. Their big chests were guarded by fourteen pairs of ribs—one more than the ox.

Vast sheets of ice not only affected the destiny of living creatures; the face of North America was modified by nature's plastic surgery. Creeping down from the general region of Hudson's Bay, ice sheets gouged out the basins now occupied by the Great Lakes. Pulverized rocks and soil scraped from northern regions, deposited at the time of melting, filled those valleys that remained after tops of hills were ground away.

Net result of these processes: formation of a new region of level, fertile land where mesquite grass flourished to form one of the world's greatest natural pastures—ideal for the hump-backed grazing animal with sharp horns and nasty disposition. Buffaloes multiplied until they became the dominant animal of the entire Great Plains area, then spread into wooded sections around the edges. Always most numerous in prairie country, bison were found in most of the United States.

It was inevitable that the thick-skinned creature should become basic to the economy of New World tribesmen. By the time of Columbus, an estimated 100,000 humans lived on the buffalo range—almost wholly dependent upon products of the hunt. All other plains animals together did not exert a fraction of the buffalo's influence upon human affairs. It is unlikely that the American Indian's dependence upon bison has been matched by any other man-animal relationship.

Clumsy in its movements and indifferent to sounds, the big animal could be dropped by a single stone-tipped arrow—provided a hunter approached from down the wind so his quarry's keen nose would not detect danger. Lacking any motive to kill more bison than could be used, Indians never took more than a few hundred thousand animals a year—hence there was no thinning of the ranks.

Tribesmen used every part of the buffalo. No portion of the meat was discarded. From the hide came moccasins, kettles, robes, and lodge coverings. Green hides were stretched over wooden frames, fashioned into boats. Hair was woven into ropes and halters. Big bones were shaped into pounding tools, while small ones furnished the Indian's only awls and needles.

Buffalo horns were made into drinking cups, knife handles, and ornaments for the war dance. Even the hoof was useful—as a mallet with which to split the skull. Internal organs were shaped into water vessels. And on the treeless plains, buffalo dung was the universal fuel. Dried into "chips," animal droppings were used to cook buffalo meat for men whose whole way of life was shaped by the creature they hunted.

An early writer, awed by the skill with which every fragment of a carcass was used, wrote of the Sioux, "they make so many things of the buffaloes as they have neede of, or as many as suffice them in the use of this life."

North and south, east and west, it was the same throughout the prairie region. Buffaloes meant existence for Sioux and Cheyenne, Kiowa and Cree, Shoshone, Pawnee, and Arapaho. Having reached a state of natural balance, men and animals lived together for centuries without significant shifts in population. Apparently, hordes of bison would roam the plains forever.

With the coming of the white man, new factors were introduced into the situation. Three of them were of such weight that, combined, they spelled the doom of the New World's most significant beast.

Biological scales were first tipped by a creature whom Europeans brought across the seas and turned loose on the plains. Small and insignificant by comparison with a buffalo, the horse is faster and more agile. More important, he is sufficiently docile to train for use with a plow—and in the hunt.

Descendants of horses brought by the Spanish became the wild ponies of the prairies. Captured and tamed by Indians, they provided the red man with a potent new resource. No longer forced to stalk his prey on foot, the warrior now rode to the buffalo hunt—and killed at a fast-rising tempo.

White hunters were not yet interested in the big animal of the western plains.

Though never abundant east of the Mississippi, bison once ranged from Virginia to New England. LaSalle recorded that in 1680 he found the Illinois prairie alive with them. Even that notable herd probably numbered only a few thousand animals. By 1800 it was unusual to see a full-grown bull or cow anywhere in the East; within a generation, the buffalo had vanished from haunts in Wisconsin and Indiana.

Half-breed trappers of the Red River country began systematic hunting as early as 1800. Eventually the annual buffalo hunt became big business in the remote northwestern region. More than 600 men made up the 1840 party; accompanied by 1210 carts, they made a foray that resulted in slaughter of about 47,000 animals.

Records of that hunt indicate that there was tremendous waste. Though the hunters took away 1,089,000 pounds of meat, three times as much was left to rot on the plains. Four or five hides were discarded for each one brought to the trading post. No longer zealous to use every morsel of each animal killed, hunters were beginning to slay in mass for the sake of choice portions of the carcass.

Even though a few hundred men killed wantonly, the bison might have held out for generations—had not the rifle and the locomotive finished the grim work begun by adding horses to the pattern of the hunt. During the Civil War, buffaloes were twice as numerous as humans in the United States; just two generations later, the Smithsonian Institution had difficulty finding animals from whom to perpetuate the species.

Hudson's Bay trade guns and muzzle-loading rifles were vastly superior to bow and arrow. But loading was a slow, clumsy process. There was a limit to the number of shots any hunter could fire in a day.

Civil War inventors and munitions makers probably gave no thought to buffaloes; they raced to devise weapons that would kill men more rapidly and efficiently. Once hostilities were over, however, the new breech-loading rifle added to the advantages of the hunter over his quarry. Armed with a .44 Remington or a .40 Sharps, a skilled horseman could drop bison with new speed and precision. Buffalo Bill Cody killed sixty-nine animals in a single eight-hour hunting day.

Given apparently limitless numbers of buffaloes on the plains and efficient tools with which to slaughter them, it is small wonder that the ranks of professional hunters grew rapidly. Just one more element was needed to complete the pincers closing upon the animal: a transportation system to move meat and hides from the frontier to eastern markets.

John Stevens was ridiculed as a dreamer when, in 1823, he proposed building a railroad from New York to Ohio and thence to "the great western lake." Interest in a transcontinental line grew steadily during gold rush days, however. While serving as U. S. Secretary of War, Jefferson Davis was a major proponent of such a project.

On July 1, 1862, Lincoln signed a bill chartering the Union Pacific and the Central Pacific Railroad companies. Less than seven years later, rails were joined at Promontory Point, Utah, to link the oceans with ribbons of steel.

As lines moved west, the pace of buffalo hunting quickened. From each new railhead, hides and meat were shipped back east. Only the best parts were used: the liver, hump, and tongue were especially prized. Buffalo meat never brought more than 3¢ a pound, often sold for $2 a ton. Tens of thousands of animals were killed for their tongues alone. Once an agent of London's exclusive Carlton Club paid a hunter $500 for 1000 tongues. That was exceptional; the standard price was 25¢ each.

Hides and robes became so plentiful that the market was glutted and prices fluctuated in the range of $2 to $3. From an estimated 125,000 robes a year entering commerce, the number multiplied many times. In 1882 the Northern Pacific alone hauled 200,000 to market. During the peak years, New York brokers made fortunes that rivaled those of old-time dealers in beaver and mink.

Frenzied slaughter was concentrated in a period of little more than a decade. While it continued, waste was so great that each ton of slain buffaloes yielded about two pounds of meat or hide that reached market. Wealthy sportsmen organized special trains, shot from car windows for the thrill of seeing big animals drop. A traveler along the Arkansas River reported that in 1873 a man could jump from carcass to carcass for fifty miles without touching ground.

That year, animals still ranged within ten miles of Wichita —which was a hunters' town. By 1886 the last buffalo had disappeared from the region.

Everywhere in the West the story was the same: incredible numbers of bison, then absolute extinction. Wealthy ranchers kept a few animals for exhibition; small herds took refuge in Canada and the Yellowstone region; a handful were sheltered in zoos. That was all. After thousands of years as master of the plains, the buffalo had succumbed to the white man's horse, rifle, and locomotive.

Bones scattered about the prairie were the only memorials. Eventually some desperate homesteader thought of sending them east to fertilizer factories. Bleaching skeletons were gathered by bone pickers and stacked into ricks at every western railroad station. Prices ranged from a low of $6 to a high of about $10 a ton. In 1874 alone, three major rail lines hauled out 20,744,000 pounds of buffalo bones.

Later analysts have concluded that the all-out war upon

the bison was not wholly motivated by economic factors. For though records of the time include few direct references to support such a view, it is clear that some whites killed buffaloes in order to sabatoge the red man's war effort.

Many whites carried a homemade poison tube for use in the event of capture by Indians. For it was clear to Sioux and Crow, Cheyenne and Blackfoot alike that every buffalo hunter challenged the red man's very existence. Resisting an 1875 political move that would have led to protection of those bison remaining in Texas, General Phil Sheridan warned: "The buffalo hunters have done more in a few months to bring about peace with the Indians than the whole Army could do in thirty years!"

Late in life, old-time hunter Frank Mayer admitted that army posts usually issued free ammunition to buffalo killers. For many a man in uniform subscribed to the view that there was no choice: in order to subdue the Indians, it was necessary to wipe out the animals on whom they were dependent.

Success was all but absolute.

Though conservationists began working as early as the 1870s, lawmakers responded slowly. Kansas and Colorado passed protective laws—after the bison was nearly exterminated in those regions. Dr. William T. Hornaday, of the New York Zoological Park, made the first accurate buffalo census in 1889. That year he reported just 1091 animals, most of whom were included in Canadian herds.

Theodore Roosevelt and other prominent outdoorsmen threw their weight behind the move to save the buffalo; preserves were set apart in national and state parks. Hence the global population of this most magnificent of game animals now hovers about the 25,000 mark.

Central in bow-and-arrow cultures, the mighty buffalo

hasn't a chance in the industrial age. Barring man's near extermination of his own species through nuclear warfare, there is no likelihood that bison will ever again be important to humans.

The Wolf: Jekyll and Hyde of the Outdoors

Ann Ronell made history, in a fashion, when she wrote a theme song for Walt Disney's *Three Little Pigs.* "Who's Afraid of the Big Bad Wolf?" she gaily demanded, and soon her defiant jingle was being sung around the world. That was all very well in 1933, for by then the four-legged foe no longer presented a major threat to civilization.

Man's long fight against his most aggressive animal enemy is rapidly drawing to a close. Now largely confined to remote northern wilds, the wolf offers only token resistance to the hairless biped against whom he has struggled for mastery of 30,000,000 square miles.

Canis lupus, the gray wolf, has exceeded most or all other wild animals in extent and intensity of competition with man. It once ranged over most land surfaces of the Northern Hemisphere—from Mexico, Arabia, and India northward to Arctic regions. No one knows its precise spread in time, which is at least as astonishing as its spread in space. On the basis of the evidence at hand, it appears that the bold killer has been abundant for much more than 50,000 years.

During the Stone Age, men and wolves probably lived together without serious friction. There was sufficient game for both. Each could normally keep out of the other's way.

Matters took a drastic turn when men settled down to till the soil and keep domestic animals. Deer, caribou, elk, and other big game were slowly pushed away from the fringes of civilization. Their natural supply of food reduced in this fashion, wolves turned their attention to livestock. They began preying on sheep and cattle some 10,000 years ago—and have been at it ever since.

Before men developed the art of writing, the wolf had become a symbol of both greed and danger. Hence some of the very earliest of Greek documents include an already ancient phrase, "to keep the wolf from the door," or stave off starvation. Seeking for the most vivid of ways in which to convey his dream of peace, the prophet Isaiah sang of a time when wolves and lambs will lie down together.

Aesop's fables, thought to date from about the sixth century B.C., reflect ancient views more faithfully than do formal histories. Though the storyteller paid lip service to the lion as king of beasts, he showed that his real deference was to the less imposing wolf. Always depicted as treacherous and terrible, the sheep killer is chief actor in thirty-seven fables.

According to the story of "The Nurse and the Wolf," Greek parents often tried to force a child to obey by threatening to throw him to the wolves. Persisting in speech through thirty centuries, the phrase is still applied to any situation in which a tender, trusting person is exposed to dangers too vast for his understanding.

Religious rites dedicated to the wolf, and proverbs about the animal, abounded among many peoples. He is the stock symbol of cunning in languages ranging from Greek and Latin to Chinese, English, Polish, Russian, and dialects of American Indians.

Wolves figured in the teachings of Jesus and the writings of such diverse thinkers as Herodotus, Plutarch, Chaucer, Milton, Shakespeare, Sir Walter Scott, and Benjamin Franklin. Hundreds of European families took their surnames from the animal, leaving literary mementos ranging from the Anglo-Saxon epic of Beowulf to exploits of the fictional detective, Nero Wolfe.

There is nothing in the appearance of the animal to indicate its key role in global competition. At a casual glance, even a 170-pound male looks very much like a big dog. By comparison with an elephant or a saber-toothed tiger, he seems weak and harmless.

Typical specimens weigh only about eighty pounds, measure some five and one half feet from nose to tail tip. Unlike exotic tropical creatures, the wolf is decidedly drab in appearance. An occasional individual shows bright colors or bold markings; most of them have off-color coats of rather dingy gray, shading into brownish and reddish hues.

Like most dogs, wolves have five toes on each front foot but only four on the hind ones. They resemble household pets in ways of wagging their tails to express pleasure, curling their lips into a snarl when angry.

But there are obvious differences. Wolves seldom make barking sounds. Instead they produce mournful howls that carry for long distances even against the wind. Their ears look much like those of dogs, but the wild creatures always hold theirs firmly erect—pricked for sounds that spell food or danger. Drooping of the dog's ear is a mark of domestication, the sign of an easy and relaxed life which seldom knows the reality of life-and-death struggle.

For individual wolves and the species, existence is a dynamic field which has chase for prey as one pole and flight from hunters as the other.

It is the incessant craving for fresh meat, preferably torn from the carcass of a still-quivering animal, that brings the wolf into conflict with man. Grouse, rabbits, ptarmigan, and other small game contribute to the greedy fellow's diet. Occasionally he even eats grasshoppers, fruits, and berries. Year in and year out, however, good red flesh is his staple.

Ancient herdsmen kept few records, so accurate knowledge of the toll levied by wolves is quite recent. Most of it has been accumulated in the period since hunters slaughtered the buffalo. Desperate for a new source of food, wolves accelerated the tempo of their raids upon flocks and herds. By 1897, careful estimates suggested that in the United States alone, take of the crafty killers was at least 500,000 animals a year—chiefly calves and yearlings. Even with steak retailing for 15¢ a pound, the typical wolf killed cattle to the value of about $1000 a year.

Exceptionally bold and cunning individuals have defied all efforts of their human enemies, while racking up incredible scores. Lobo, "the king," gained wide renown as leader of a wolf family which ranged throughout most of New Mexico. During a five-year period, the big outlaw killed at least 2000 cattle. He usually selected yearling heifers, ate only the most tender parts of the carcass. In six years prior to 1920, the Custer wolf raided South Dakota ranches singlehanded. His estimated take: livestock worth $25,000.

In southern Arizona, one noted killer outwitted all hunters for eight years—meanwhile taking an average of two calves a week. Sometimes he went on a spree of wanton slaughter, butchered fifty sheep in a single night. Old Three Toes, perhaps the most famous of the U.S. wolves, raided South Dakota ranches for thirteen years. At least 150 men tried to kill or capture him. He was finally taken in his old age in the year of progress, 1925. His record, which may be an all-time high: sheep and cattle worth more than $50,000.

No other animal has ever approached the wolf in extent and intensity of competition with man in his roles as hunter and herdsman. In past centuries not only grim and bloody contests for big game and domestic animals took place, but also struggles in which human lives were at stake.

Most present-day experts believe that wolves avoid attacking members of the human race. There is abundant evidence that this has not always been the case. During centuries when wolves were more plentiful and men had less effective weapons, the fierce animals were constantly pressing their two-legged foes. An appetite for human flesh may have been abnormal and occasional. But there is strong reason to believe the man-eating wolf of the past to have been no fictional creature, but as real as the man-eating tiger of the present. "Little Red Ridinghood" is a literary fossil which points to actual conditions during many centuries of European life.

Wolves are notoriously fond of carrion. Scrambling for rotting bodies in ancient tar pits, large wolves of a now extinct type were sometimes trapped and their skeletons preserved.

Taste for human flesh may have developed from feeding on battlefield carrion. As late as the time of William the Conqueror, says an early chronicle, it was not unusual for commanders to leave dead bodies on the field—to be devoured by wolves and vultures. On their long flight from Russia, Napoleon's veterans were followed by large numbers of wolves.

Some of them were seen as far south as the borders of the Rhine.

Saxons gave the present month of January a name equivalent to *Wolfmonth.* According to some authorities, the title grew out of the fact that attacks on humans were most frequent at this time of winter. As late as the mid-point of the sixteenth century, say early Scottish records, it was necessary to provide lodges to shelter travelers from prowling wolves.

It is all but impossible to separate fact from fiction, but recent centuries have seen several eruptions of violence by man-eaters. One of them, Courtaud—or "Bobtail"—preferred human flesh to beef or mutton. In 1428 he is said to have invaded Paris itself and killed a victim not far from Notre Dame cathedral. Three centuries later another French monster was credited with the death of more than a hundred persons, whom he attacked and overpowered one by one. King Louis XV eventually led a nationwide search involving 43,000 armed men and some 4000 dogs. After seven weeks, the biggest hunting party in history killed the black-faced "Beast Wolf" which had terrorized the whole Rhone Valley for three years.

Some naturalists discount all such stories on the basis of the belief that human flesh is distasteful to wolves. Yet a few accounts are too recent to be regarded as legends. As late as 1924, the Rome correspondent of the London *Observer* joined the debate. In the chaos following World War I, said he, wolves multiplied in Italy to "an alarming degree." He stated that there had been several cases of attack on humans —in one of which the killers gorged on the body of the victim.

Controversy over details of wolf lore is not limited to past or present dietary habits.

For generation after generation, intelligent and responsible civilized people swore that humans were often changed into werewolves. This belief was well established as early as the time of the Greek historian, Herodotus. It has been found in practically every part of the world where men have come into contact with wolves.

Medieval Europe was the scene of frequent and frenzied panics over the fearful beast whom early English had named from combining *wer* (man) and *wulf* (wolf). Danes vowed that any man whose eyebrows met was certain to become a werewolf. French, German, Lithuanian, and Slavic traditions had many elements in common. Any child born in a strange fashion—say, feet foremost or with teeth—could easily be transformed into a wolf-man. Normal folk subjected to witchcraft could suddenly assume the manners and much of the appearance of a wolf.

Such beliefs are too widespread and too prolonged to be dismissed as sheer fancy. They probably grew out of distorted understanding of common phenomena.

Some types of insanity doubtless contributed to the werewolf complex. But the most potent factor may have been prevalence of rabies among the prowling killers. Any person bitten or scratched by a mad wolf was likely to contract the fearful disease—and hence begin to exhibit many traits somewhat like those of wolves. American Indians lacked an understanding of rabies, but were aware that it sometimes swept through wolves of a whole region. In periods when it was prevalent, infection of at least a few humans was almost certain.

If the werewolf mystery has been solved by better understanding of natural processes, that is far from the case with the greatest riddle of man-wolf relationships. Throughout recorded history, there have been rare but persistent reports of cases in which human infants have been reared among wolves.

One of the earliest is the world-famous story of Romulus and Remus. These legendary founders of Rome were said to have suckled a wolf-mother who adopted them in babyhood.

Many scholars scoff at the tale, trace it to mistaken identification of the nurse's name, Lupa, with that of the wolf, *lupus*. If that is the origin of the story, the mistake was made very early. One of the finest art objects surviving from the sixth century B.C. shows two babies nursing at the breast of a stalwart wolf. Etruscan in origin, this magnificent cast bronze testifies that ancients swallowed their wolf stories whole.

During comparatively recent centuries, there have been at least fourteen other reports of the wolf-children. Twelve of them come from India, where Kipling used the idea in the story of Mowgli—the wolf-boy who was the prototype of Tarzan and all other animal-reared heroes of modern literature.

Most tales of four-legged foster parents are automatically suspect because of insufficient data. That is not the case with the best-known and most recent of them.

According to his detailed account, the Reverend J. A. L. Singh saw two girls running with a wolf family on October 9, 1920. Since he operated an orphanage well known in his section of India, the missionary decided to rescue the children. He hired native hunters, who dug into the anthill which constituted the den of the wolves. Adult animals were driven off or killed; cubs were given to the natives. Singh captured two girls whose ages he estimated at eight and two years.

Subsequently named Kamala and Amala, the wildlings showed few human traits. One died within a short time; the older girl survived for nine years. Singh made numerous photographs and voluminous records which were later studied by experts. Many of them respect his sincerity but doubt his conclusions, feeling that the children were mental defectives not actually reared among wolves.

Other distinguished scholars, including the child psychologist Arnold Gesell, believe Kamala and Amala were actually stolen by a mother wolf and reared with her pups. Unless new cases are reported and analyzed in the future, there may never be general agreement as to whether or not wolves have occasionally served as foster parents of human children.

On the question of their economic threat to civilization, there is universal agreement. For at least 3000 years, perhaps longer, there has been a price on the head of the wolf.

In the great age of classical Greece, the lawmaker Solon established a bounty of five drachmas for a male, one drachma for a female. Many a feudal baron maintained special wolf hunters at his own expense for the protection of his serfs. About A.D. 965, the Saxon king, Edgar, settled a national brawl in terms of scalps. As a condition for peace with the King of North Wales, he demanded annual tribute of 300 wolf pelts. Three centuries later, English rulers were still making land grants based on the owner's promise to work for the destruction of the swift marauders.

Within a decade after the Pilgrims landed at Plymouth Rock, bounty acts were launched in North America. Revisions and new laws have continued for 300 years.

Rewards for taking a wolf have included sheep, hogs, grain, wine, rum, lead, powder, money, and tobacco. By an act of the Assembly, in 1646 Virginia offered 100 pounds of tobacco for each wolf killed. Ten years later, Rhode Island required each resident Indian to pay annual tribute of two wolf skins—in lieu of taxes.

Bounty payments mounted rapidly after 1850, continued

to high levels as late as World War I. Historians estimate that in the United States alone, various branches of government have paid out at least $100,000,000 in rewarding wolf killers.

Yet it would be possible to support the view that, over the long haul, wolves have more entries on the credit side of the ledger than on the debit side.

Direct contributions to man have been meager. Several tribes of Indians ate wolf flesh, and it has saved the lives of a few hungry trappers and explorers. During the winter of 1806, Meriwether Lewis and his party were reduced to a diet that included wolves. But the meat has never been really significant as a source of human food.

Wolf pelts are not of size or quality to compete with the great commercial sources of skins and leather. As late as the time of Elizabeth, many English dignitaries trimmed their robes with wolf fur. But this fur was chiefly ornamental rather than useful. A few wolves have been tamed and forced to pull sleds or perform other work. The importance of their contribution at this point is negligible, however.

Quite a different situation prevails when the indirect influences of the animal are assessed. Few if any other creatures have given so much to the humans against whom they have fought so long.

Most authorities believe every single strain and type of dog in the world is descended from some ancient kind of wolf. It was once believed that the jackal was the immediate ancestor of the dog; new understanding of dental structures in all three animals suggests that the real link is between dogs and wolves.

Paleolithic cave art, some of it thought to be 50,000 years old, shows Stone Age hunters accompanied by canines—almost certainly tame or half-tame wolves. Long association with man led to changes in both habits and bodily structure.

As a result, the dog evolved as man's first domestic animal. It is still so wolf-like that interbreeding occurs readily.

Chaldean and Egyptian relics show that man had developed a number of distinct types of dogs as early as four or five thousand years ago. Since then, breeding experiments have produced so many specialized kinds that no other animal shows such varied forms.

By the irony of nature, the wolfhound and other fierce dogs helped men hold their own against the wolf. And in ancient times the dog's contribution to success in hunting may have tipped global scales which gave hunters the leisure to begin planting crops.

Whether or not success with the dog helped men to think of domesticating other creatures is anybody's guess. It remains an intriguing speculation. So does the possible role of the wolf in the evolution of early sheep and cattle. Just as is the case with modern populations of bison, elk, mountain sheep, and other big game, ancient herds and flocks must have included some weak specimens. By preying upon them, leaving the most fit animals, wolves may have speeded the development of strong and healthy domestic animals—which, in turn, became bases on which civilizations were erected.

Man's victory over the wolf is incredibly recent, when seen against the backdrop of the long global struggle. Only the cutting and burning of forests made the win decisive. Reduced to dwindling havens in the Far North, the wolf's present importance is negligible. In terms of total human development, the scope of its dual role has been too vast for measurement.

The Fly That Came to Dinner

William Oldys, who knew nothing of the germ theory of disease, once grew sentimental watching a fly sip from a cup of ale. So about 1750 he issued a standing invitation:

Busy, curious, thirsty fly,
Drink with me, and drink as I.

That is precisely what the housefly has been doing for centuries. Long ago he became a self-invited guest at the tables of man. He likes this arrangement so well that he shows every intention of prolonging his visit indefinitely. All efforts to oust him are stubbornly ignored. He has a good thing and doesn't intend to give it up.

Indeed, he has acquired the status of an undesirable visitor only recently. Houseflies and men lived in mutual tolerance for an estimated 10,000 years; mounting tension grew into open conflict only half a century ago.

Early history of the buzzing marauder is obscure. Having no bony parts, he cannot be studied from skeletal remains.

Lacking typical insect habits, he did not succeed in becoming trapped—and preserved—in amber. Due to his minute size, he was not selected as a model by ancient sculptors and artists. So scattered literary references give our only clues to his past.

These sources are vague, for they do not include enough details for positive identification. A plague of flies helped persuade Egyptians to release Moses and his followers, but there is no certainty that houseflies rather than some of their cousins were involved. Both in ancient Syria and classical Greece, there were religious ceremonies dedicated to one or more kinds of flies.

In spite of inconclusive evidence, most authorities believe the housefly has been abundant for a long, long time. He probably became attached to man about the time our common farm animals were domesticated. Until the beginnings of modern scientific medicine, no one considered him an important actor in the drama of civilization.

Late in the sixteenth century, the noted Mercurialis observed that flies passed freely in and out of plague-ridden homes. He suggested there might be some vague connection between the insects and the disease, but no one took him seriously. Two centuries later an investigator accused flies of spreading tropical ulcers, or yaws. Since he was unable to prove the charge, it remained buried in obscure scientific works.

During the Civil War, a prominent American physician became suspicious of the fly and proposed a study of its role in the communication of disease. No one bothered to act on the suggestion until 1896. L. O. Howard, a noted entomologist working for the U. S. Department of Agriculture, undertook the first thorough investigation. He quickly found that the insect divides its interests between filth and human food, made a heroic effort to persuade the public to change its name to "typhoid fly."

Even his findings might have gone unheeded, had it not been for staggering military losses. Flies were responsible for one epidemic after another during the Spanish-American War. And fly-spread typhoid proved more deadly than guns during the Boer War.

Stunned by the sudden realization of the fly's lethal role, U.S. crusaders launched a frantic campaign. There was a terrific flurry of publicity and activity. Chautauqua lectures and schoolroom drills had as a goal, not control, but elimination. To the tune of "Battle Hymn of the Republic," boys and girls marched about singing:

The filthy fly is flying in a flight that's strong and fleet;
He carries germs and microbes in his mouth and on his feet;
Let us swat the dirty insect with a blow that's swift and neat,
While he is flying on.

Reaching a peak about 1910, the anti-fly campaign achieved considerable success in Europe and the United States. Meanwhile, medical research was developing better methods to prevent fly-borne ills. Though it never subsided entirely, public interest began to wane. Men prided themselves on having practically won the battle against the insect, forgot it in concern over wars, depressions, communism, and nuclear fission. Though the 1953 edition of the *Encyclopedia Britannica* includes twenty-three volumes of a thousand pages each, the housefly merits only half a column.

Half tolerated as minor pests, each of these visitors is actually a minute buzz bomber. It is anybody's guess as to whether the much discussed H-bomb actually poses a greater threat to mankind than does the tiny invader who is sometimes beaten in skirmishes but has never lost a campaign.

At least thirty disease organisms may be carried by flies. Tuberculosis, typhoid fever, cholera, yaws, and trachoma are best known. On the global scene, however, diarrhea and enteritis probably wreak most havoc. No other cause of infant deaths is more important than fly-spread intestinal infections which rage annually in many lands. Even in the relatively protected United States, the cost of illnesses spread by flies is estimated at $69,000 a day—every day of every year.

Had a battery of engineers set out to design a machine to transport bacteria, their device would not approach the fly's efficiency at the job.

One observer has described the insect as "a flying brush." Its entire body is covered with minute hairs. This coat of thatch, ideal for sheltering microscopic hitchhikers, extends even to the legs, feet, and wings of the insect. Flies captured in sanitary areas may carry up to 100,000 bacteria on their bodies; Cox, Lewis, and Glynn found flies from filthy districts to carry as many as 500,000,000 bacteria.

Many of these are carried on the insect's six elaborate feet. Each is equipped with two soft pads covered with a thick coat of hollow hairs. Sticky fluids ooze through the hairs, provide sufficient traction to permit the fly to walk on windowpanes and ceilings. But when he explores stable manure or sewage, his pads become so clogged that he strews debris behind at every step when he stalks through the sugar bowl or across the breakfast toast.

That is just the beginning.

Not only is the housefly a two-winged brush; he is also a flying tank car. Due to the structure of his mouth parts, he is unable to feed upon solids, so he greedily sips almost any liquid containing organic matter. His preference runs toward such staples as serum from animal dung, pus, cesspool seepage, moisture from around the eyes, sputum, perspiration, nectar, and milk.

But beggars can't be choosers; when he can't find suitable food, he manufactures his own on the spot. Seizing a grain of sugar or other soluble matter, he vomits on it. When the prize has dissolved, the fly sucks up the droplet—unless he is disturbed before he finishes.

Familiar "fly specks" are more likely to be vomit spots than excreta. Some of them stem from the gluttonous habit of eating rapidly, then retiring to a quiet spot to regurgitate and sip at leisure. Others result from interruptions during the process of softening up a tidbit. These two factors cause the typical housefly to produce about fifty-five vomit spots each day.

Were nothing but food involved, the fastidious would condemn the fly's table manners. Since he feasts on all types of fermenting and decaying matter, his crop is usually well stocked with bacteria. No matter how many he stuffs into his belly, his health is affected only by a special virus. Disease organisms which are fatal to humans can live in his stomach and intestines without causing him the slightest inconvenience. Hence the outer surface of the typical fly's filth-plastered body carries only a fraction as many bacteria as he hauls in his stomach—ready to spray upon food at any instant.

How many disease organisms the adult insect carries over from early phases of his life cycle no one knows. There is evidence that the number may be considerable.

Flies invariably deposit their eggs in putrid or fermenting material. Pearly white and slightly curved—somewhat like a banana—the egg is barely visible to the naked eye. Within a day it hatches and produces a transparent grub. Other cycles of development follow rapidly; three times, in as many days, the growing maggot bursts its old skin and forms a new one.

Resources of science have proved inadequate to solve some of the riddles connected with the grub's brief life. It is not known, for example, what the tiny creature eats. Some experts think it feeds upon micro-organisms that thrive in such material as damp manure, rotting fruit and vegetables, kitchen garbage, and decaying animals or slaughterhouse waste. Other analysts believe the maggot eats nothing except chemicals produced by fermentation and decay.

Whatever its diet may be, the legless larva develops rapidly. After reaching the third stage, an unknown hormone or other chemical initiates complex changes. Within a period as brief as six hours, the skin contracts into a barrel shape and turns brown. Incredibly rapid changes take place in the confined organism. Entering its case as a grub, under favorable conditions it emerges as an adult fly within two days.

Even the method of escape from the capsule is a triumph of nature. In order to push the end off its case, the fly inflates an air sac. Forced from a narrow slit between the eyes, this organ breaks open the confining shell. Then it is withdrawn, deflated, and never used again.

Crawling from its case with wings folded in tight pads, the fly buzzes away as soon as it dries. From the moment it emerges, it is an adult. There is no change in size, though weight may increase. Already infested with bacteria absorbed during the maggot stage, the newly launched engine of death darts off to feast on dainties which man provides in careless abundance.

Food is not the only bait which attracts flies to men, but it is among the most important. Having no mechanism to bite or chew, the housefly spends his life on a liquid diet.

Suitable juices are not abundant under natural conditions, but abound wherever man is found. So long as it is soft enough for him to eat or capable of being dissolved in his own juices, the fly is willing to dine on almost any animal or vegetable product.

Fortunately for the insect, man has made sweeping alterations in the environment. Droppings of wild animals are usually scattered so widely that they dry quickly. Man brings creatures together into flocks and herds, carefully piles manure into juicy heaps that are just right for maggots. Industrial development has reduced the number of small barnyards. But there are abundant dairies, hog pens, garbage piles, slaughterhouses, sewage disposal plants, septic tanks, and other choice spots for incubation of the fly's eggs.

Additional advantages stem from man's ability to control temperature. Flies thrive only in a narrow heat band—from about 45° to 110° F. Nature offers few shelters from winter ice, summer heat. But man erects buildings which temper both extremes.

Except in tropical zones, survival of the housefly may depend upon shelters provided by man. Individual insects probably do not live long enough to hibernate through the winter. Without some spots in which new generations could be reared, the species would be threatened with extinction. Dairy barns and other shelters permit year-round breeding. With the coming of warm weather, the enormous fecundity of the insect can result in hordes of descendants from the few who were produced during winter.

A fourth major contribution by mankind to fly-kind is protection from natural enemies. Numerous creatures would prey upon flies if man did not drive them away. No civilized person will permit lizards or other amphibians to live in his house. Spiders and toads are killed by the squeamish. Neither the dragonfly nor the praying mantis is encouraged to hang around merely to feast on flies. Wasps and centipedes are smashed on sight. Insect-eating birds visit the haunts of man only occasionally and in small numbers.

The total effect of these factors is enormous. Man literally creates a special environment which is ideal for the multiplication of the fly. He provides abundant food, a wide variety of materials in which larvae may develop, shelter from extreme temperatures, and protection from enemies. In the natural state, houseflies would have a constant struggle to survive in small numbers; fleeing to man's bosom, the insect has found it easy to breed by the billion.

Fifty years of vigorous attack upon the housefly have thinned its ranks a bit—especially in Western lands. Yet all the skills of man have proved inadequate in the fight against the insect invader.

Many experts predicted that automobiles would exterminate flies—for horse manure was long the chief breeding ground. But as the horse population dropped, flies turned to other types of fermenting filth and entered the gasoline age with undiminished vigor.

Early experiments with sticky flypaper and poisoned bait raised hopes that were soon dashed. So did the initial success of chemical sprays, soon after World War I. DDT, whose potency was accidentally discovered, was hailed as invincible. A few enthusiasts gaily predicted that the housefly would soon be as rare as the dodo.

DDT was first used on a wide scale in 1947. In Iowa, health authorities spent $500,000 on an all-out campaign that promised to rid the state of flies. U.S. occupation forces hoped to exterminate them in Italy. Efforts in Idaho were so successful that scientists had difficulty finding specimens to use in experiments.

Within months there came a growing chorus of puzzled reports. Some flies survived DDT, reared hordes of descendants who resisted the potent chemical. Such hardy strains were reported from Italy, Sweden, Denmark, California, Ohio, and Alabama. In 1948, the degree of resistance was termed "alarming." Next year, a survey showed 87 per cent of Illinois farms to be infested with DDT-resistant flies. By 1952, the National Pest Control Association was warning that summer would bring "a worse plague of flies than at any previous period in recent times."

Though the fact of resistance to DDT and other insecticides is well established, its mechanism is far from understood. Several sets of factors may be involved.

Individual insects with special but unknown traits have been observed to survive doses that kill their fellows. They rear broods that seem to become increasingly hardy over a period of several generations. One experimenter bred flies so tough they couldn't be killed with insecticides—so he had to take away their food and let them die of starvation.

Such developments have revived old arguments about the effect of environment upon heredity. No one actually knows whether insecticides stimulate genetic changes or are merely defeated by already resistant individuals. This much is certain: having developed immunity to DDT over a period of two or three years, flies were able to overcome new chemicals in two months. Some experts hoped that resistance would disappear when exposure to insecticides was reduced. Apparently that is not the case; it has persisted through as many as thirty unexposed generations.

New chemical weapons, used singly and in elaborate combinations, have proved more potent than DDT. How long any one of them will give effective control is an open guess. Most analysts now agree that there will never be a substitute for sanitation. Insecticides can supplement but not eliminate a continuous campaign to deprive the fly of man-provided places to breed and feed.

Entomologists term the insect *Musca domestica,* "domesticated fly." Most members of its family are parasites upon other insects. Hence one specialist considers it "probably the most beneficial single family of insects known." Conjecture has it that the housefly itself once deposited its eggs in or upon other insects. Eventually it abandoned these food sources in favor of the ferment heaps of primitive man.

If this theory is correct, the fly has probably undergone biological changes during hundreds of generations of dependence on man. Some of its early features may have been lost in the same fashion that domestic sheep have shed their horns. Hence this insect has no body parts with which to distribute pollen, kill or injure its winged competitors. Today's houseflies are so completely adapted to a man-made environment that they couldn't leave it if they tried. A continuous and vigorous campaign will not drive them away but can keep them under reasonable control—provided there are no radical changes in the conditions of civilized life.

Under global warfare with new explosives, the housefly could surge to crucial importance. For this flying guest has several advantages over its host.

Humans usually produce one offspring at a time; flies seldom lay less than four or five batches of 100–150 eggs each. Men mature slowly, require some seventeen years to reach adulthood. Flies can make the cycle from egg to adult in about ten days. Given ideal conditions, it has been estimated that a single pair of flies could produce 191,010,000,000,000,000,000 offspring between April and August. Allowing one eighth cubic inch per insect, these would cover the earth forty-seven feet deep.

Such estimates are well laced with fantasy, for existing conditions never even approach the ideal. But bombed cities without sewers or water mains, lacking adequate insecticides, could become giant fly incubators. Under conditions of total war, the fly's germ-teeming droplets could be more deadly than man-made bombs.

Entomologists most familiar with its equipment for distributing disease have suggested that, even in time of peace, it is a major achievement for man to succeed in co-inhabiting the planet on which the insect lives. Having prepared a table at which the housefly is pleased to sit, man must remain eternally on the aggressive in order to prevent his guest from becoming master of the house.

Nature's Strangest Chemical: Milk

Milk is so familiar to modern Americans that most take it for granted. Actually, it is both a biological rarity and a chemical marvel.

In all the vastness of the cosmos, there is no certainty that living organisms exist anywhere except on Earth. Confined to narrow zones about the planet's crust, life manifests itself in at least a million forms. Of these the vast majority—996 out of every thousand species—are incapable of producing a single drop of milk.

Practically all organs, glands, and systems manufacture chemical compounds linked with digestion, metabolism, respiration, elimination, and reproduction. Milk is in a class all by itself. It is the only large-scale organic secretion that has no known connection with needs of the creature who makes it. Alone among a myriad of fluids and solids formed by plants and animals, milk is produced by one individual for direct consumption by another.

There are many theories, but no real explanation, for the

fact that milk has a special place in the scheme of things. Mammals take their name from Latin *mamma*, or "breast." They were the last major class of creature to develop, emerging a mere 150,000,000 years or so in the past. All mammals have warm, red blood and a four-chambered heart. From elephant and bat to mouse and whale, every species breathes air.

But the mammal's most unusual traits are associated with the development and nourishment of its young. With only a few exceptions, they form within the mother's body. Until birth, all nourishment is provided by her blood.

Late in pregnancy, an elaborate hormone reaction leads to changes in the mammary glands. Soon they begin to secrete a fluid that is delicately balanced to meet the full dietary needs of the infant. How the wizardry takes place has long been a puzzle. Aristotle pondered the problem, gravely concluded that milk consists of "parboiled substances from the blood."

Two thousand years of study have given more data, yet the Greek's judgment still sounds strangely modern. For no analyst fully understands how materials taken from blood and lymph are transformed into milk. Mother animals eat a great variety of foods. Though proportions differ somewhat, all kinds of milk—regardless of the mother's diet—have about the same basic constituents.

Nature not only manufactures the queer stuff; she also provides efficient ways to get it to its destination—the stomachs of hungry young ones. Mammary glands vary in number from one to twenty-two pairs; creatures who bear large broods have the greatest number of teats. No matter where these organic spigots are placed on her body, the mother knows how to give them to her babies.

Most rodents lie down while the young are nursing; most

cud-chewing animals stand. Wild rabbits even sprawl on their backs to feed their babies. Australian anteaters never have to give the matter a thought. Milk oozes continuously from breasts and collects in the pouch where their young are carried; they, in turn, lap it up any time they feel hungry. Quite a different type of efficiency is seen in the bottle-nosed dolphin. Swimming slowly, the mother turns on her side. As soon as the baby's mouth touches a nipple, the parent contracts a muscle and squirts out a stream of milk with such force that an entire feeding is completed in a matter of seconds.

Most experts agree that the provision of milk represents a special triumph of biological forces. In general, the "higher" the evolutionary level of a creature, the more helpless are its babies. An amoeba just formed by cell division is fully equipped for life; it has no period of infancy. But seven months are required for a blue whale to reach a state in which it can eat in adult fashion.

So milk is a necessity during the formative period of young mammals. The length of the suckling period varies widely. Few small rodents nurse for more than three weeks. Seals rely upon their mothers twice as long, while humans require mother's milk—or a substitute—for a year or more.

If he lives to maturity, man becomes the most powerful of Earth's creatures. But before he can put his huge brain to work, he must pass through periods of infancy and childhood that greatly exceed those of any other form of life. Lacking a special food suitable for his helpless stage, no baby of ancient times could have survived.

Just when humans began to feed their young with milk produced by females of other kinds it is impossible to determine. Nor is there any way to find out how this radical idea was conceived. It may have arisen from an emergency. Lacking a human or animal wet nurse, the infant whose mother died was automatically condemned to death. And when two or three babies were born within a brief period, a supplement to the mother's milk was urgently needed.

Some modern primitives place their orphan babies directly to the teats of milch goats; among a few peoples, reindeer herdsmen suck their does, though they do not know how to milk. The actual milking of animals by hand is a far more complex act than nursing from a four-legged foster mother. So it was probably a comparatively late development. The earliest definite record is a temple frieze uncovered in Ur of the Chaldees. Thought to date from more than 6000 years ago, it depicts one man milking and another who appears to be churning.

Once the use of non-human milk was discovered, it spread rapidly in that part of the ancient Near East that is sometimes called "the cradle of western civilization." Egyptians thought so highly of it that they depicted the heavens as an animal with distended udders. Greek poets began to use milk as a symbol for abundance. Hebrew tribesmen who invaded the land of Canaan were partly motivated by a belief that it was so fertile it could only be described as "flowing with milk and honey."

Religious beliefs and ceremonies came to be intimately linked with the life-sustaining fluid. Sacrifices were made to cattle in both Egypt and Greece. In the latter region it became customary to make a special offering—a heady brew of sour milk, honey, and water—to the demons of the nether world. An early Greek ceremony included the verbal formula, "I fell into milk"; whether this involved actual baptism in it is uncertain. In regions as remote as Britain, milk played a major part in worship.

Funeral rites of many cultures involved use of milk. Both

in Greece and Rome, mourners poured the precious fluid on the ground. Celts are thought to have washed their dead with milk—a practice still commemorated in a European children's game which has a refrain running, "Wash them in milk and clothe them in silk."

Early Christianity did not escape the influence of general reverence for milk. Some churchmen gave the convert a cup of milk and honey after baptism; others substituted it for wine in the communion feast. Though formally outlawed by action of a church council in A.D. 692, these practices persisted in some regions as late as the ninth century.

Use of milk as a food was probably restricted to infants and children, for it was scarce and perishable. Ancient herdsmen could get it only a few months each year, during the season after young were born. Their only containers were skins that were never washed. So in hot climates, milk soured very rapidly. Some of it was eaten as curds; crude types of butter and cheese were made in many regions.

All dairy products were considered to have medicinal value. As late as the second century A.D., the great physician Galen thought butter to be useful only as a remedy, especially for burns and other skin injuries. Wealthy women sometimes used it to dress their hair, just as the wife of Nero enjoyed the luxury of bathing in asses' milk. Newborn babies were frequently washed in milk—which was probably more hygienic than much water of the period. Hippocrates prescribed the white fluid as a cure for tuberculosis, and Arabian physicians used the milk of camels as a general remedy.

Milch cows were scarce and unimportant. They do not thrive in hot lands, nor can they eat the coarse food that is suitable for some milk producers. Ancients were glad to get milk from any source. Some were especially skillful in rearing goats, but sheep's milk was widely used. As late as the fourth century, Europeans regarded it as the most important kind. Men of the era did not hesitate, however, to use milk of mares, asses, and camels. Kumiss, a fermented drink made from mares' milk, was a staple food of the Huns who overthrew the Roman Empire.

Cows began their rise to prominence less than a thousand years ago. By 1100, they were beginning to lead in producing dairy products other than such specialties as Roquefort cheese—still properly made from the milk of ewes.

Taken to Britain and Scandinavia, milk cows flourished in the colder climate. Production rose, and dairy products gradually became important articles of commerce. Since butter kept comparatively well, it came to be a standard item for the larders of ships. Various kinds of cheese were perfected, and a few bold thinkers began experimenting with selective breeding in their herds.

Few histories of England even mention milk, but it played a major role in the developing nation. By the thirteenth century, dairies had become so significant that Milker was in use as a surname. London already had a Milk Street in this era, and herdsmen of Guernsey could talk with pride about the special strain of milch cows they were developing.

Men could and did sneer at a spiritless fellow as a "milksop." But when the first Europeans came to the New World and found it without a milk animal, they hurried to supply the deficiency. Spanish adventurers brought cows to South America quite early in the sixteenth century. English settlers shipped them across the North Atlantic prior to 1611. On her second voyage to Plymouth, the *Mayflower* herself brought three heifers and a bull. An important source of human food for only a few centuries, the milch cow came into her own in the new land of rich grass and mild weather.

Once launched, bossy's rise to prominence has never been

halted. Other milk producers have dwindled in importance while the cow has risen. Unless otherwise specified, almost any present-day reference to "milk" can be taken as dealing with that of the cow. Reindeer, camels, water buffaloes, asses, mares, and sheep still produce small quantities of milk for human consumption. Goats are of some significance in limited areas.

On the global scene, however, the cow reigns supreme. In a single year, modern dairies process more milk than was consumed during the entire history of the Roman Empire. In the United States alone, some 23,000,000 milkers yield more than one hundred fifteen *billion* pounds of milk every twelve months. A vat big enough to hold one year's milk from U.S. cows would have to be ten feet wide, ten feet deep—and 3600 miles long.

As she functions today, the dairy cow is actually a mobile chemical plant. Raw materials which enter the factory consist of grass, hay, and prepared feeds. Along with considerable quantities of water, these ingredients are placed in the cow's rumen, or paunch. Thirty or forty gallons in capacity, it serves as a fermentation chamber.

One-cell organisms which thrive in the warm paunch break down original compounds and build many new ones. From simple compounds of nitrogen, they synthesize complex proteins. Organic acids and B vitamins are also manufactured.

Already greatly modified from the form in which they entered the chemical plant, quantities of proteins, fats, and minerals enter the cow's blood stream. Rushed through pipelines of her body, they reach her udder. This department of the factory is actually a huge skin gland. Exclusive of milk, it may weigh as much as sixty pounds. It consists of secreting glands, lymph channels, milk ducts, veins and arteries, nerves, muscle, skin—and fibrous connective tissue.

Altogether remarkable in its own right, the udder extracts a great many materials from the cow's blood and lymph. Exact measurements have never been made, but some experts estimate that blood surges through a good milker's udder at the rate of 200 pounds an hour. Others insist that this figure is far too low. In order to yield her twelve gallons a day, they suggest, a champion cow may have to pump 6000 gallons of blood through the system that makes up her department for assembling the finished product.

As delivered into the pail, milk has a most elaborate physical structure. It is a solution of sugar and mineral salts in water. At the same time, it is a suspension of undissolved protein particles. And to complicate the matter still more, it is an emulsion of fat globules.

Ancient milkmaids had no notion of the fluid's intricate structure. They knew, however, that when permitted to sit for a time, milk separates into two layers—of which the top one is rich and oily. They also knew that when milk sours, thick curds form in the bottom of a bowl, while watery whey collects on top.

Scientific study of these matters was launched in 1674. That year, milk was examined through the microscope by the great Van Leeuwenhoek. He didn't learn much, but wrote his friends in London that he had seen tiny globes of fat in fresh milk. Much later, these bodies were measured. Size varies considerably; 8000 average ones, laid side by side, would stretch a distance of just one inch.

As early as 1899, a French analyst conceived the idea of breaking globules into such small sizes that they would not rise to the top and form cream. His idea led to homogenization. Modern plants force milk through minute openings at a speed of sixty miles a minute; hitting metal surfaces, fat particles shatter. Reduced in size, they are held by electrical and molecular forces—so remain dispersed all through the milk instead of coming to the top. So the quart of homogenized milk on your breakfast table contains billions of microscopic droplets of natural oil.

Casein, which forms curds when milk sours, includes many complex proteins. No one knows precisely what their nature may be. But, somehow, the vats and retorts and reaction chambers of the cow do manufacture chemicals whose formulas may be as elaborate as :

$$C_{9490}H_{13425}N_{2160}O_{2640}S_{45}P_{45}$$

Minerals—concentrated largely in casein—usually include potassium, calcium, phosphorus, sodium, sulphur, iron, copper, manganese, zinc, and iodine. By 1948, analysts listed 101 recognized components of cow's milk.

One of those constituents, lactose, or milk sugar, is of special importance. It is found in every kind of milk yet analyzed—and nowhere else in nature. Hence it is sometimes described as "the strange sugar made especially for the feeding of young mammals."

High in energy and easy to digest, it appears to have some mysterious connection with mental activity. For the lactose level of milk seems to vary according to brain weight of the species involved. Lactose makes up only 6 per cent of the dry matter in rabbit's milk. In cow's milk, the concentration is six times as high. And the dry matter of human milk is 56 per cent lactose—far more than is found in any other source.

Investigators have hardly scratched the surface in the study of milk production, composition, and digestion. It is recognized, for example, that exposure to sunlight leads to chemical reactions in milk; their nature and effects are unknown. Much evidence suggests that human milk includes an anti-polio substance—but how it gets there is anybody's guess.

Experiments in modifying the composition of milk by controlled feeding are in their infancy. Yet the opportunities are real, for radioactive iron appears in milk within five minutes after it is fed to a cow. Most tastes and odors of food substances are eliminated or modified. For some puzzling reason, wild onions and garlic begin to taint milk only sixty seconds after they enter the cow's mouth.

Regardless of the riddles of the chemical processes that take place in the cow and other milk makers, this much is definitely established: the complex fluid is the most satisfactory known food for humans. There is too much water in it to permit large-scale consumption. Besides, milk is low in some vitamins and in such essential minerals as iron, copper, and manganese. Even so, no other substance is a close rival for the title of "man's best food."

The study of nutrition is a young discipline; there was no effort to measure the caloric value of foodstuffs until 1885. Clear recognition of the role of vitamins followed four years later. By 1900 it was generally conceded that there are qualitative as well as quantitative differences in the value of food components. Milk ranks high by all quality standards. Large-scale use of whole milk and milk fractions by adults is a very recent development. No matter how desirable, it would have been impossible in earlier eras. As it is, precise conditions for production and distribution in quantity do not yet exist outside North America and western Europe.

Numerous complex and interlocked changes were required before milk could become a global—or even a national—staple.

At first, one of the most significant of them had no obvious connection with milk. Louis Pasteur, challenged to find a way to stop spoilage of wine, learned that heat will arrest fermentation. Announced in 1864, his findings helped lay a basis for the germ theory of disease and for the heat-treatment of milk.

Actual pasteurization of milk was not perfected until after the scientist's death. Nathan Straus, the philanthropist, in 1893 opened a station for the distribution of heat-treated milk to impoverished children of New York. By 1906, an estimated 5 per cent of the city's milk supply was pasteurized. Not until 1921 did the sale of raw milk cease in the world's largest city.

Progress in other urban centers was comparable. As late as 1932, however, controversy still raged over the basic idea. Many dairymen insisted that raw milk tasted better and was more nourishing. At that time, about two thirds of the milk sold in U.S. communities under 10,000 was untreated. As late as 1946, 2100 of the nation's towns and cities had no pasteurized milk.

Development of milk sanitation and sterilization actually grew out of a grave problem: raw milk was tried in the court of medical research and found guilty of transmitting many maladies.

Sale of milk was first forbidden in 1599. That year, physicians charged that an epidemic was due to the use of dairy products, though they had no idea of the exact process involved. A serious outbreak of septic sore throat in Kensington, England, was traced to milk in 1875.

The year 1895 brought the first rumblings in the United States. That year, the health commissioner of Washington, D.C., hinted that much illness among children might be associated with milk. A report of New York's city board of health, 1896, includes what is believed to be the world's first reference to dangers which stem from bacteria in milk.

Subsequent study has shown that milk is an ideal food for

many tiny organisms as well as for men. It comes from the cow at 101° F.—a temperature ideal for the multiplication of bacteria. No matter how carefully it may be drawn from healthy animals, milk already contains micro-organisms before it reaches the bucket. Careless handling invites contamination from the hands and clothing of the milker, air of the stable, and the utensils in which the fluid is handled.

Samples of commercial milk taken in New York City in 1907 showed an average of 70,400,000 bacteria in each teaspoonful. Under present federal regulations, raw milk with less than 50,000,000 bacteria per quart is entitled to be labeled "Grade A." A bacteria count of 50,000,000 to 1,000,000,000 per quart covers the category of "Grade B." Milk with more than 1,000,000,000 bacteria per quart is termed "Grade C."

From the health standpoint, the number of bacteria in milk is all but meaningless. What matters is type, not quantity. Bacteria and molds operate to form buttermilk, cheese, and butter. Though the role of these tiny organisms was not recognized until 1872, few favorite dairy products can be made from sterile milk.

Whether their influence is beneficial or deadly, bacteria often multiply very rapidly in milk. If stored at room temperature, the rate of increase may be incredibly fast. Milk with an initial count of a few thousand bacteria a quart can be seething with tens of millions within a day.

Until modern techniques were developed, milk was the most dangerous of foods. Not only did it spread typhoid fever, diphtheria, scarlet fever, septic sore throat, and similar ills; tuberculosis and other maladies of the cow were passed to human consumers. Bovine tuberculosis has come to be recognized as a major threat to man's welfare only in the present century. Large-scale attacks upon it were launched about 1910. In the United States, the disease has been practically eliminated—but the conquest required thirty years and some $275,000,000.

In order to bring milk into general use, it was not enough to make it clean and safe. Sweeping changes had to take place in handling, transportation, packaging, and the economics of dairy farming.

Beginning late in the last century, a wave of inventions transformed the handling of milk. A cream separator was perfected in Sweden. Various kinds of milking machines were devised; by 1903, one of them was proving generally satisfactory.

Until very recent decades, practically all milk was consumed by the producer or by adjacent families. There were no devices to ship it any distance. After London's population grew past 1,000,000, much of her milk supply came from cows stabled within the city. New York housed 18,000 of the animals in 1840.

Rail shipment to the city from outlying dairy regions began in 1842, expanded rapidly. Eventually urban centers came to be served by special trains running from the country daily. Such a "milk run" was usually early in the morning; flexibility of scheduling came only after refrigerator cars entered general use. Milk was first shipped in a tank car in 1910, a tank truck in 1914. Today the familiar ten-gallon milk can is rapidly becoming obsolete for bulk shipment.

The actual production of milk has changed almost as much as the handling of it. Cows of the Middle Ages yielded only a few quarts of milk a day, less than six months each year. Most of their output was required to feed their own calves.

Selective breeding, practiced for several centuries but only recently intensified, has led to the development of cows who specialize in manufacturing milk. "Dual purpose" animals—reared for both beef and milk—have not proved satisfactory.

Dairymen get best results from using such milk breeds as Brown Swiss, Holsteins, Jerseys, Guernseys, and Ayrshires. The formation of special herds of such animals has become general only since 1880.

Tremendous dividends—in fluid form—have resulted. In the generation after World War I, U.S. cows increased 15 per cent in number; meanwhile, milk production rose 50 per cent. The development of artificial insemination promises an even faster rate of change in the quality of herds. Today the typical scrawny mongrel of India yields about 350 quarts of milk a year. U.S. cows produce four times as much, while those of Holland average 3500 quarts annually.

Some of the increase has come from genetic changes, but part of it stems from radical new feeding practices. Under natural conditions, milk production dwindles to a trickle or ceases entirely in winter. William Pynchon, of Massachusetts, is believed to have been the first commercial producer to practice stall-feeding. He gave his animals grain and hay during winter, found he could milk them all year.

Use of the silo became general about 1890. Since then, numerous experiments have led to such practices as feeding ground corn, soybean meal, bone meal, beet pulp, molasses, and other specialties.

Many of these changes set other developments in motion. Gathering mass and momentum, the trend toward quantity production and handling led to the industrialization of U.S. milk. Packaging has undergone one change after another; milk is now canned in several forms, dried, and even frozen for storage.

Strangely, war has had a major impact upon the rate of these changes. Condensed milk was established during the U. S. Civil War; evaporated milk gained much ground during the Spanish-American War; and dried milk was greatly aided by World Wars I and II. Lacking a powerful incentive such as war, there is no assurance that capital funds would have been invested to permit the costly "tooling up" that is essential to industrialization. Soldiers and refugees who tried new forms of milk by necessity almost always continued to use them after hostilities ceased. So, in a single century, milk changed from a fluid produced on a small scale for home consumption to a major article of world commerce.

Bulk processing and new forms of milk have greatly reduced costs. Powdered milk can be shipped across the Atlantic for the sum required to transport whole fresh milk a distance of ten miles. American preferences for such products as butter and cheese have led to huge surplus stocks of other milk fractions. Hence non-fat dry-milk solids have been distributed to peoples of other lands in vast quantities.

This is a very recent development in world nutrition—a side effect of the surplus produced by the booming industrialized dairy economy of a few Western nations. India has more cattle than any other country of the world, but her milk yield is low. South America, Africa, eastern Asia, and Indonesia are just beginning to use milk. In some lands, climate is such that milch cows do not flourish; in others, religious views and cultural traditions have impeded the dairy movement.

As late as 1930, per capita use of whole milk by the Japanese was less than half a gallon a year. Military defeat, economic distress, and malnutrition created a vacuum just right for a change in food habits. Hence in 1954 the Japanese government purchased from the U.S. government the fabulous quantity of 10,000,000 pounds of dried milk.

Agencies of the United Nations have distributed free milk in many regions where it was never commonly used before. Western capital has been invested in processing plants around the globe: a bottling plant in French Morocco, pasteurization equipment in Venezuela and Ireland, heavy machinery in Guatemala and Malta. In 1953 the hit song among natives of the Belgian Congo was a tear-jerking ballad telling how powdered milk from the West saved the life of a Bantu youngster whose mother had no life-sustaining fluid in her breasts.

Barring wars which will bring the industrial age to a chaotic end, everything points to still more remarkable progress in the future production and use of milk. A few nations of milk users have developed since 1800; as the tempo of change grows more rapid, it appears that two or three generations will see a planet of milk users.

Even laboratory wizardry in the creation of synthetics does not threaten to challenge milk in the foreseeable future. For the incredibly complex fluid is more than the best food known. It has indirect effects just now beginning to be investigated—but perhaps as important as direct food value. Milk serves as a culture medium for bacteria in the human intestines, hence has a catalytic effect upon other items of diet. No one yet knows precisely why, but the nutritional value of white flour rises about 50 per cent when eaten with milk. The biological value of corn is nearly doubled when milk accompanies it on its journey through the human digestive system.

Designed by nature as a special food for young mammals, milk was essential to the development of the human race. Comparatively late in biological history, men conceived the idea of eating part of the milk which domestic animals manufacture for their own young. Developing very slowly for several thousand years, milk entered a new era when the cow won prominence as a dairy animal. Selective breeding and scientific feeding boosted the production of milk; reaction to

Pasteur's germ theory of disease made it safe; transportation and packaging underwent a series of revolutions.

Man has successfully diverted the course of biological processes without which he could not have achieved manhood. Today calves get only one out of every thirty-three quarts of milk produced by cows in the United States. Fresh whole milk, butter, cheese, condensed milk, evaporated milk, ice cream, cottage cheese, dried milk, and milk fractions are bringing a new era of health to the diverse peoples of Earth.

Recognizing that it is more than a poetic metaphor to say that modern civilization is a ship sailing on a sea of milk, no man can fully understand all its complexities. At best, we can recognize with Thomas Edison "the Almighty knew his business when He apportioned milk. He is the best chemist we have."

The Lacquered Lady Who Kills for Men

Lady bird, lady bird! Fly away home!
Your house is on fire; your children do roam!

Lifting lacquered wing covers and taking flight under the prodding finger of a child, the oval-bodied creature appears as daintily feminine as any member of the insect world. Actually she is a professional killer whose tastes are such that her banquets help provide an adequate food supply for mankind.

Many species have been familiar to Europeans during this entire era. Because they were long regarded as enjoying the special protection of the Virgin Mary, they came to be known as ladybugs or ladybirds. The economic importance of the insect family was not recognized until recent generations.

First discoveries were made quite by accident.

Prospectors who settled in California quickly stripped the land of its major gold deposits. Then they found that an even greater golden yield could be harvested from citrus trees. Early growers made quick fortunes. Then a new insect enemy appeared: cottony-cushion scale. Small and inactive, it feeds on sap from leaves and soft twigs.

Some citrus groves were infested as early as 1872. During the next dozen years, the invading insect spread through the West. Many trees died and thousands were so severely injured that they yielded no fruit. Detective work by orchardmen traced the pest to importations of financier James Lick —for whom the famous observatory was later named. Lick had brought cuttings of the flowering peach from China; apparently they were infested with tiny sapsuckers then unknown in the Western world.

By 1893 horticulturists were beginning to find occasional specimens along the Atlantic coast. Five years later, the havoc wreaked by aphids was so serious that the German emperor issued a decree forbidding importation of American fruits or living plants of any type.

C. V. Riley, chief entomologist of the U. S. Department of Agriculture, suggested that aphids could be controlled by introducing other insects which would prey on them. In 1890 that proposal was so radical that even many of his close associates scoffed.

Working against both indifference and open opposition, Riley set out to find some creature that would attack the aphids that thrived on citrus trees. He found a clue in the fact that the insects did little harm in Australia; evidently some natural enemy was keeping them in check. Why not send his brilliant young assistant, Albert Koebele, to find and bring back an Australian insect that would save the orange industry?

Officials in Washington nodded as they heard the plan outlined. Yes, it certainly seemed logical. But the Department of Agriculture had no funds for foreign travel. Taxpayers would certainly protest so extravagant a venture. It would have to be abandoned.

By this time Koebele had his jaw set. He refused to take the rebuff as final and managed to persuade the State Department to send him to the Melbourne Exposition as an official representative!

Reaching Sydney late in 1888, he recruited a team of Australian scientists as aides and quickly discovered a tiny fly that is parasitic upon scale insects. Almost it seemed that his job had been too simple. Elated at its success, he shipped thousands of flies back home.

Official records do not reveal precisely what set of circumstances prevented his immediate departure for California. Somehow he was detained in Australia. So during the enforced visit, he continued to study the scale insects in their native habitat. Quite by accident he discovered that a reddish-brown ladybug seemed to have a special appetite for eggs and larvae of the scale. Actually, the insects preferred these items to anything else available on the Australian menu. Perhaps it would be a good idea to send a few of them to America.

By the time they arrived, Koebele's associates were sure that the parasitic flies would fail to stem rising tides of scale insects. If thousands of these wee killers were useless, what could one hope from twenty-eight ladybugs?

Yet they were placed on infested trees and watched. Several other shipments arrived soon afterward. By March 1889, California was host to precisely 514 Australian ladybugs, or *Vedalia*. They thrived at once, multiplied so rapidly that within two years scale insects were under control throughout California's citrus regions.

Since then, various types of ladybirds have been established in more than thirty nations. Without exception, they have reduced or eliminated the damage of scale insects which infest orange and lemon trees.

Success of the ladybird experiment was so dramatic that it marked an era in scientific agriculture. Since then, there have been hundreds of attempts to find insects which will control insect pests or noxious plants. Economic entomology, now a major operation around the globe, grew directly from the rescue of California's oranges by the lacquer-covered insect.

Though new in its role as protector of man's food supply, the bright flier had long been familiar to countryfolk of several lands.

Just how it came to be known as Our Lady's Bird no one knows with certainty. Pious folk of the Elizabethan era endowed many common creatures with names having sacred associations, it is true. But most such terms were local in character. In the case of the ladybird, another factor was involved. Far from being a colloquial name employed in a few districts of England, it was found in many languages in closely related forms.

Germans called the wee creature *Marienhuhn, Marienkäfer,* and *Marienwurmchen.* And earlier, the slang term *Marienkuh* flourished as an equivalent of the English *Ladycow.* Swedish scholars used the name *Marias Nyckelpiga,* while farmers of that land still call the insect "The Virgin Mary's Golden Hen." A slightly different emphasis is found in French and Spanish, where the name links the creature with protection of God the Father. French call it *la bête à bon Dieu,* and Spanish use the name *Vaquilla de Dios.*

Neither coincidence nor cultural exchange is sufficient to explain so widespread a view concerning an insect. Scientific names, usually in Latin, are common to many nations. But it is extraordinary for folk names to be so closely parallel.

Why should persons in so many lands regard the beetle as enjoying the special favor of the Virgin Mary?

There is only one reasonable conjecture.

If you grew up in a rural district, you undoubtedly know that birds and animals almost always leave the ladybird strictly alone. Long proficient at chemical warfare, the insect manufactures a yellowish fluid which it discharges in time of danger. Joints of the leg are so fashioned that they rupture under slight stress and release drops of serum. Though seldom noticed by humans—whose sense of smell is blunted—this liquid is highly offensive to foes of the ladybird. Consequently, the bright insect goes about its business in virtual immunity from attack.

Early observers, amazed at the beetle's sheltered and charmed life, probably concluded it to enjoy the special favor of the Lady whom they venerated and whose beneficence they sought. So it was natural to call the insect Lady-bird. English dialects included such variant titles as Lady-beetle, Lady-clock, and Lady-cow. Standardization of speech made these names obscure, and gradually people abandoned capitalization of the initial letter. Hence it is only the pious who continue to find in the insect's name a monument to earlier reverence.

Yet the findings of modern entomology were anticipated by farmers of Elizabethan England. Though they did not understand the economic significance of the ladybird, some folk probably realized that it feeds upon other insects. Hops, long a major crop in the island kingdom, are vulnerable to attacks of plant lice. Hence ladybirds abounded in hop fields and may have been observed more carefully than lack of written descriptions would indicate. Until 1861 scientific literature included no mention of the fact that ladybirds feed on the aphids which infest hops.

Folk literature preserves some special clues, however. Instead of using the abbreviated version familiar to U.S. youngsters, children of several European lands know and recite a longer form of the rhyme:

Lady-bird, Lady-bird, fly away home!
Your house is on fire.
Your children do roam.
Except little Ann, who sits in a pan
Weaving gold laces as fast as she can.

As every boy and girl knows, that rhyme must be recited after a ladybird has been placed upon the outstretched index finger. That the custom has changed little through the centuries is indicated by a woodcut which dates from the reign of King George II, and shows a child addressing a ladybird.

Though it seems to have more rhyme than reason, the jingle takes on new significance when viewed against its historical setting. Farmers frequently gathered hop plants and burned them after harvest was over. Since ladybirds abounded, children enjoyed the game of warning the little creatures to flee from danger. "Little Ann" was the farmer's title for a young grub of the beetle, cemented to a leaf and engaged in shedding its skin—or "weaving gold laces."

Modern observation indicates that the young insect actually goes through several radical changes. Five days after waking from her winter hibernation, the adult beetle lays a dozen or so eggs. Shaped like tiny tapered needles, they are fastened to a leaf by cement from the body of the mother.

Less than a week passes before the eggs hatch. Young who emerge from them bear no resemblance to adult ladybirds. Stretching its six folding legs, each larva sets out in search of a meal. It will eat almost any type of plant lice: aphids, thrips, and other soft-bodied insects that can be mastered by the grub-like attacker. After two weeks of gorging upon plant parasites, the growing ladybird becomes dormant. Attaching itself to a leaf or a stem by the tip of its abdomen, it draws itself into a ball and then sheds its skin. After a second transformation, it steps out in adult form.

Resembling a round pill cut in half, the adult is seldom more than one fourth inch long. Colors range from black with red or yellow spots to red or yellow with black spots. *Coccinellidae,* scientific name for the insect family to which it belongs, stems from Latin *coccinus* (scarlet).

More than 2000 species are known. Not all of them include scarlet markings, but most varieties can be identified by the polka-dot pattern. Spots vary in number from two to twenty-two, usually remain fairly constant within a given species. These markings appear on the elytra, or protective coverings, which shelter the filmy wings of adult insects. Australian beetles which serve as guardians of citrus trees differ from their European and American cousins by showing irregular black striations rather than distinct spots against the red background.

Two members of the family, marked by sixteen and twelve spots, respectively, seem to deserve the title "lady." That is, instead of living by the slaughter of other insects they prefer vegetable diets. But one is especially fond of beans and the other thinks no food compares with leaves of the squash. Familiar to us as the Mexican bean beetle and the squash beetle, these two varieties are the only ladybirds that reduce man's food supply rather than protecting it!

Once scientists discovered that nearly all ladybirds are natural foes of plant parasites, great numbers of them were reared in special insectaries. They have centered in the Pacific coast area of the United States, for it is this region that has seen the world's most costly attacks by aphids and scales. In the Pacific Northwest alone, parasitic insects damaged fruit and trees to the tune of $20,000,000 a year in the period just after World War I.

Large-scale propagation and distribution of ladybirds was a major factor in control. During 1919 alone, farmers of a single state—Washington—released about 100,000,000 ladybirds in groves and fields.

Some varieties fly to the mountains in late fall, gather in great clusters, and hibernate until spring. Consequently, there developed a considerable business in gathering and storing the insects for sale the following year. L. W. Higgin, of Dobbins, California, has adopted the business slogan: "Don't Spray! Destroy Aphis Nature's Way."

O. B. Lester, of Sonora, has gathered millions of ladybirds for shipment by air. His volume of business is exceeded only by that of George C. Quick, of Phoenix, Arizona. Having devised methods to keep the beetles in cold storage during winter, Quick both gathers his own crop in the mountains and acts as a wholesale merchant—buying and selling ladybirds gathered by others along the slope of the Rockies. Retailing his insects in two-gallon lots of about 270,000 individuals, he sold an estimated 3,000,000,000 during his first fifteen years in business.

These men and their associates, as well as many scientific entomologists, declare that the ladybird will never lose its usefulness. A far more efficient killer than any poison yet devised, the beetle abounds under natural circumstances. Those reared and transported by men account for only a tiny fraction of each year's brood.

At least 350 varieties have established themselves in the United States. Their protective work of killing for men has important effects upon the world's economy. Without the ladybird, it is doubtful that growers could produce substantial crops of major fruits.

The Pig:
Self-Propelled Packing Plant

Foodwise, man is the most versatile and experimental of creatures. Life can be sustained on anything from an all-vegetable to an all-meat diet or any combination in between. Humans have learned to enjoy every type of meat from woolly mammoth to rattlesnake, from dog to prime steer. Most quadrupeds now living have been hunted or bred by various tribes and peoples. Yet on the long-range global scale, all other meat animals combined do not equal the pig's importance as a factor in human development.

Virtually a packing plant on four legs, the modern porker is not only a cornerstone of civilization; he is also a biological mystery. For no one knows precisely what combination of factors prepared the prehistoric digging animal for his role in human nutrition.

Ancestors of today's wild hogs and purebred show animals ranged through tropical swamps of Europe and Asia an estimated 40,000,000 years ago. During subsequent epochs, the animal's descendants have undergone remarkably little skeletal change—less than any other domestic beast.

Earth had no grasses or nut-bearing hardwood trees until

very late, as time is measured by the geological clock. So for millions of years hogs were forced to subsist on low-calorie forage. Much of their diet probably consisted of coarse tubers and roots of plants growing along watercourses.

It was during this period that the animal's most distinctive piece of equipment served to keep him alive. No other creature has a structure quite like the snout of the hog. Projecting from his skull in direct line with the thick neck and main part of the body, the snout is actually an efficient digging tool. Though quite sensitive to touch, the leathery pad which includes both mouth and nostrils is just right for stirring up mud and soft earth. Added strength is gained from a unique pre-nasal bone—a prism-shaped body just in front of the bones of the nose, and connected with them by cartilages and muscles.

Primeval hogs were equipped to dig out food from areas not accessible to most of their competitors. And they had just the kind of digestive apparatus needed to process large quantities of coarse provender: a small, simple stomach plus some seventy-five feet of intestines.

On the basis of these factors, it would seem logical that the animal should thrive in swamps and river courses. All the evidence of archaeology indicates that this was precisely the case. No fossil swine have been found in either desert or plains country; many bones have been found in regions of ancient rain forests.

For muddy sectors not only yield food under the probing of snouts; such an environment is just right for the hog's strange thermal system. A thick-skinned creature, or pachyderm, he has limited capacity to throw off excess body heat. So he wallows in mud to keep cool in summer. Far from having the warm coat of a bear or buffalo, the pig is insulated with only scattered bristles that give him little protection against the cold of winter. This factor, which accounts for the high incidence of respiratory ills among domestic swine, greatly restricts his climatic range.

Designed by nature for a life in swamps and humid forests where many creatures would starve, today's wild boar is less belligerent than his early ancestors. Yet even the modern specimens are armed with weapons of combat as well as gear for digging.

Each jaw includes twenty-two teeth, of which the canines are most highly developed. All these eyeteeth project beyond the lips. Those of the lower jaw curve backward and upward. Opposite teeth in the upper jaw—unlike those of typical animals with tusks—do not curve downward. Instead they loop out and up before turning inward. Comparatively short upper tusks rub continually against long, sharp ones beneath, so the boar whets his weapons every time he chews a mouthful of food.

Tossing razor-sharp tusks with all the might of his muscular neck, a half-ton boar is among the most dangerous of animals. After years of stalking big game, Sir Robert Baden-Powell named hog hunting as the most thrilling exploit of his experience—a sport he considered more dangerous than tiger shooting. In reaching that judgment, he simply echoed the verdict of earlier hunters.

"There is neither lion nor leopard that slayeth a man as a boar doth," wrote Edward of York in his noted volume on *Master of Game*. According to the fifteenth-century authority, "the wild boar slayeth a man at one stroke as with a knife." Writing a few decades earlier, Count Gaston de Foix reported that he had often seen hounds, horses, and huntsmen "cut to ribbons by great tusk teeth of boar."

Few creatures have been hunted by so many notables. Long a royal sport in China, the boar hunt was a favorite diversion of Kublai Khan, who followed trained leopards rather than dogs. Boars were hunted by generations of Roman generals and emperors—including Trajan and Constantine. As late as the close of the fifteenth century, this dangerous form of the chase was followed by Pope Leo X. Barehanded mastery of a boar was among the major exploits of Hercules, but the hero Adonis was slain while hunting one of the animals.

Armed with a rifle and mounted on horseback, the modern big-game hunter thinks twice before he pursues a boar into a thicket. Afoot and bearing nothing more formidable than a club or crude spear, men of the Old Stone Age hunted boar for the sake of their succulent flesh.

It was hunters, say some theorists, who took the first step toward reducing the beast to a sorry state of slavery. According to this view, Neolithic spearmen sometimes killed a sow whose babies were small and helpless. Reared in captivity, they reproduced and gradually became reconciled to living about man's camps and settlements.

Other authorities hazard a somewhat different guess as to the way so fierce a creature became domesticated. It was his stomach, they insist, that led to subjugation of the hog. Hungry animals found it easy to gorge themselves at primitive garbage heaps or kitchen middens. After a few generations of hanging about to get man's scraps, swine grew fat and lazy—and, for the sake of guaranteed square meals, began to breed in captivity.

Had the pig been more selective in his diet, early and primitive men would have had trouble providing food on a year-round basis. But a healthy specimen will thrive on almost anything edible. With little partiality, he crams down roots, weed stalks, tubers, grass, nuts, eggs, snails, worms, mice, grasshoppers, and the like. Far from refusing food that is rotting or infested with maggots, the hog gulps it down readily—and does not balk even at animal or human excrement.

Though seldom engaged in killing for food, the typical boar readily feeds on almost any type of carcass. In a noted case of mass murder, an Indiana farm woman disposed of her victims by throwing their bodies to her hogs.

Whether lured into domestication by a nagging appetite or tamed as a result of other factors, swine were closely associated with men at least 7000 years ago. Early centers of pork production were the grain belts of China, Egypt, and Mesopotamia. *Sus scrofa,* the wild boar, seems to have been domesticated in several independent regions. Strangely, none of his close relatives has submitted to man's rule. Failure has met every attempt to domesticate the wart hog, African forest hog, New World peccary, and babirussa of the East Indies.

During most of man's period of mastery, his grip upon the one pig he could tame has been comparatively loose. Both in Asia and Europe—and in the American colonies at a much later period—swine raising was long a forest activity. Herds of a few dozen animals roamed about in semi-wild fashion, feeding on acorns and beech mast. Their keepers did little more than watch them to prevent straying.

Swine abounded in the thick forests of ancient Britain, and were still numerous at the time of the Norman Conquest. As towns grew larger and trees were thinned, free grazing of pigs was restricted. Disappearance of Europe's public forests meant that the farmer had to feed his animals from the produce of tilled fields. Partly to prevent damage by rooting and partly to guard valuable livestock, the pig was confined first to the barnyard and then to his own tiny pen.

Since he never protested about the quality of his rations so long as the quantity was ample, it became customary to fill the hog trough with scraps, slops, and refuse. Thus the once-fierce animal of the wild was reduced to life in a pen, more strictly confined and less carefully fed than any other domestic beast. So restricted, his sharp toes and strong snout quickly turn the typical pen into a mudhole. Though clean under natural conditions and filthy only in captivity, the hog's name has entered common speech as a label of disparagement.

Some groups of men have gone so far as to place a ban on the eating of pork. Hygienic and aesthetic factors may have entered into such decisions. But the chief source of anti-pork sentiment seems to have been reaction against ancient religious practices.

As early as the Bronze Age, various tribes and peoples paid homage to their chief meat animal. Reverence for the beast reached a height among the Egyptians, who made elaborate pig images more than 5000 years ago. Sacrificial slaughter of unblemished animals by means of a sacred sickle was a major feature of worship in Roman temples dedicated to Jupiter.

Origin of the Jewish refusal to eat pork is lost in antiquity. Originally, it probably represented a firm repudiation of Egyptian beliefs and rites. In order to dramatize their independence from the gods of the Nile, Moses and his people may have declared the holy pig to be taboo for use in the pot as well as the temple.

Long before the time of Mohammed, many Arabs and Syrians took the same stand. Hence the refusal to eat pork became a deeply entrenched religious conviction, held by an articulate minority of the world's people. British disregard for this taboo set off one of history's biggest uprisings. Moslem soldiers who refused to use lard in greasing their rifles were punished, so launched the Sepoy Mutiny of 1857—which broke the 250-year rule of the East India Company.

Far from scorning pork, typical European explorers and adventurers regarded it as a staple. Even when standards of cleanliness are low, it is easily preserved by drying, salting, or pickling. Soldiers and seamen relied on it for their wars and expeditions, transported vast quantities of sowbelly and fat back across land and sea.

Queen Isabella insisted that Columbus take the familiar beasts of Europe to the New World. So on his second voyage, his cargo included eight live pigs. Liberated in Cuba, they multiplied and spread throughout the West Indies. Hence later conquistadors found a ready supply of fresh meat waiting for them when they reached the region.

Pigs arrived on the mainland in 1519. Lacking facilities to take along barrels of salt pork, Cortés had his men drive herds of pigs along their line of march. This method of moving provisions on the hoof proved so satisfactory that it was followed by many later expeditions.

Pigs reached North America with the earliest settlers. Like his ancestor, the European wild boar, the typical animal of this period was hardy and self-sufficient. He was heavy-boned, long-legged, and long-bodied. His narrow back was bent into a high arch. Large and very active, the razorback matured slowly and produced narrow hams.

Such a woods hog required little care. He could forage for himself, grow fat on acorns, roots, mast, and the like. Wild enemies gave him little trouble; an adult could hold his own against wildcats and even a lone wolf. When a pioneer moved West, he followed the example of Cortés and took his pigs along—on foot. Thriving in vast forests, pigs multiplied so rapidly that Tennessee alone reported nearly 3,000,000 head in 1840. Kentucky and Ohio were not far behind.

During the next ten years, a series of radical changes made the woods hog obsolete. For as settlers pushed into the Midwest, they discovered a region that seemed designed by nature to become the pork center of the world.

Large-scale production of meat animals demands an elaborate set of interlocking factors. Favorable climate plus abundant grass make the La Plata region of South America the finest beef country in the world. Numerous natural advantages give New Zealand the edge over all competitors in lamb production. Maize, or Indian corn, proved the key to large-scale hog culture. Pound for pound, corn turns out more units of pork than does wheat, barley, milk, or any other common foodstuff. The soil and climate of the central Mississippi Valley are just right for corn—and the region is not too cold for pigs to thrive.

Pioneers were quick to take advantage of this opportunity. Just ten years after the first U.S. hog census showed Tennessee far in the lead over any western region, farmers of the Middle West claimed four times as many swine as all the eastern states combined. Cincinnati was dubbed Porkopolis because 1833 saw 85,000 hogs slaughtered or packed in the city. Two decades later, the annual kill had climbed to 360,000. Military demand for pork brought 608,000 hogs to Cincinnati in 1863.

Old-timers shook their heads in amazement and whistled when such figures were discussed. Yet their grandsons have seen the stream of corn-belt pork expand into a world-circling flood. Meat from the pig is now used by American housewives at a rate exceeding the total from cows, sheep, poultry, and all other animals combined. In a typical year, U.S. exports include about 1,000,000,000 pounds of lard plus 1,250,000,000 pounds of pork.

This level of production rests on the encounter between an abundant food supply and a creature whose make-up can be readily manipulated by man. Lacking a crop that yields calories at low cost, it would not be profitable to mass produce hogs. Given rich food in great quantity, changing tastes could not be met by products of a living meat factory with fixed habits and rigid structure.

Naturally plastic rather than inflexible, the pig has repeatedly yielded to man's manipulations. So the cumulative effect has been to modify his ways in more radical fashion than any other common animal.

Wild representatives of the family are active, swift-moving, and fierce. Pen-fed cousins are lazy, slow-moving, and docile. Fat replaces muscles when corn is found without effort in the trough as a replacement for roots and acorns garnered laboriously.

Tusks of the boar have diminished greatly during generations of captivity. Back and sides of the modern hog are longer than those of his ancestors, while his flanks and hindquarters are deeper. Ears are less movable than those of wild relatives whose lives may depend upon their keen hearing.

Feeding habits have been transformed fully as much as the menu. In the natural state, all pigs lie in wallows or holes during the heat of the day. As night falls, animals go out to forage over a wide range—eating on the move, and frequently covering many miles before returning to the lair for another day of sleep. Domestic pigs have adopted the eating schedule of their masters—stuffing themselves by day, and sleeping by night.

Even the reproductive pattern of the four-legged meat engine has been radically altered. Wild sows produce one litter each year, suckle their offspring for many weeks. Long after her brood of three to five young ones have given up milk in favor of solid food, the mother defends them against attacks of such enemies as the fox and jackal.

A modern brood sow on a midwestern farm literally spends

her life in bringing babies—for she is more prolific than any quadruped except the rabbit. Her first litter includes four to ten piglets; subsequent ones average eight to twelve—though as many as twenty-two have been produced at a single birth. Three days after her eight-week babies have been taken from her in an enforced weaning, the sow will submit to the boar. So in a routine year she is likely to produce five times as many young as one of her wild ancestors.

Rate of growth has been altered in equally dramatic fashion. In the natural state, a boar's tusks remain immature until he is past two years of age. He attains full size in three or four more years, may live to be twenty-five or thirty.

Typical animals reared for the slaughterhouse die under the knife at four to six months. Born with eight teeth, the suckling pig can be fed a large ration of solid food within minutes after he is born. For the next two months, he gains at the rate of a pound a day; if he survives half a year, he will have increased his birth weight by 6000 per cent. Within five months after birth, a litter of ten well-fed pigs is transformed into a solid ton of pork-on-the-hoof.

Great fecundity, combined with rapid growth, means flexibility in meat supply. During war and other times of emergency, the size of the crop can rise with dramatic speed. In 1939, U.S. production of federally inspected pork was 5,600,000,000 pounds. For the next five years, the annual rate of increase was 800,000,000 pounds—to a 1944 high of 9,500,000,000 pounds.

Many of the changes in the life patterns and bodily structure of the pig have come about as a result of man's selective feeding. Human guidance of reproduction has been an equally potent factor.

Late in the eighteenth century, European hog fanciers became interested in animals from China and Siam. Crossbreeding produced the famous Berkshire strain. Attractive and sturdy, it was exploited for the show ring as well as for the farm. During the period 1830–60, breeders paid great attention to markings of animals—and placed a premium on an individual whose ebony body was punctuated with four white feet, a white splash on the face, and a white tip of the tail.

Henry Clay dabbled in hog breeding, imported four red Spanish shoats for experiments on his Kentucky farm. Daniel Webster bought breeding stock of a similar type in 1852.

During this period, every farmer was eager to help develop a better lard producer. Transportation was slow and salt pork was in great demand, so the more pounds of fat an animal could show, the better. Established about 1860, the Poland China breed became the world's most efficient device for taking corn to the packing house. With barreled pork high on the list of commodities in world trade, Iowa and Nebraska breeders produced 1200-pound boars and 900-pound sows so fat they could hardly walk. It seemed that man had achieved an all-time high in his successful effort to modify the savage wild pig of swamp and forest.

Then public tastes changed. Several factors contributed to the shift. Refrigeration eliminated the necessity for bulk use of salt, while reduction in the size of the family and transition from farm kitchen to city kitchenette created a demand for smaller hams and chops. In effect, this meant that the biological machine geared for big cuts and much fat became suddenly obsolete. Unless a new model could be produced, the animal seemed likely to go the way of Aunt Susie's quilting parties.

But the much-modified pig yielded to man's new demands. Within a few generations, descendants of lard-type animals were yielding twelve-pound hams along with less fat but more loin and bacon sides. Today's carcass provides 80 per cent dressed meat—as opposed to the 50–60 per cent of cattle and 45–55 per cent of sheep. Less than 10 per cent of the typical pig is lard, while his body is 18 per cent ham and 16 per cent bacon.

Except for his two-legged master, the pig is the most abundant large animal. World population levels fluctuate somewhere in the region of 200,000,000. More than half are found in China and the United States, though breeding is global in temperate and sub-tropical regions.

Alone among the creatures whose will has been broken by man, swine are practically useless so long as they are living. Ancient farmers along the Mediterranean sometimes drove their hogs over newly sown wheat, so seeds would be trod into the ground rather than stolen by birds. Modern searchers for truffles in untilled regions of France and Spain sometimes train sows to root them up.

But these are conspicuous exceptions. Unlike the cow, the pig gives man no milk. Unlike the sheep, it yields no wool. Unlike the horse, it provides no labor. Except among a few primitive peoples, it has not been generally considered to be desirable as a pet. So by and large, the only good pig is a dead pig.

Restricted to a single role in his contribution to the upright creature who has come to dominate the planet, the pig has performed nobly. Held captive by his stomach in order that he may fill the stomachs of his masters, he now enjoys rations that are mixed with scientific precision. He gets the best of medical care, including hormone shots and wonder drugs—without so much as paying premiums on Blue Cross policies. Veteran breeders predict that within a few generations he's sure to spend his life in an air-conditioned pen. Small wonder, then, that an observer of the planetary struggle to fill the bellies of pigs and men might be tempted to wonder who has really won the contest.

The Mexican Boll Weevil: Glutton with a One-Track Mind

Homo sapiens, Earth's eternally dissatisfied creature with a creative mind, is forever tinkering with the organic complex that surrounds and includes him. Over the long haul, his rearrangements usually give him a boost in his struggle for survival. But the changes he launches sometimes lead to trouble because chains of connection prove unexpectedly elaborate.

Such has been the case in man's dealing with a little insect whose fondness for cotton pollen knows no bounds. After many centuries of obscurity, *Anthonomus grandis* surged to world prominence almost overnight. According to Dr. U. C. Loftin, agricultural research specialist, in just over sixty years it has affected our nation's social and economic life to a degree unmatched by any other six-legged creature.

Most persons in the civilized world are familiar with the name and reputation of the Mexican boll weevil; even veteran cotton farmers are likely to hesitate and begin stammering when asked to describe their tiny foe. For a superficial examination reveals nothing startling. Body make-up is quite similar to that of some 1800 other species of snout beetles that are native to North America.

So it is small wonder that the first scientific description of the weevil created only a tiny ripple of interest. Catalogued in 1843 by a Swede whose specimens were sent from Mexico, the listing was made in the name of academic rather than practical concerns.

As late as 1885 it was too obscure to have a common name in English. That year, Dr. C. V. Riley reared a few specimens for laboratory study. His insects came from maturing seed pods, known to farmers as "bolls." It seemed logical to label them from their place of development. Insects actually infest tough-walled bolls only as a last resort; they much prefer "squares," or immature flower buds. But by the time this was recognized, *boll weevil* was established so strongly the title couldn't be changed.

According to the best guess, the insect entered Texas in 1892. For the next thirty-one years, it spread through the U.S. cotton belt, pressing into nearly 20,000 square miles of new territory each season. On some of the most fertile land in the nation, production of lint dropped from two bales per acre to one bale per fifteen acres. Economists calculated that at their peak, direct and indirect costs of weevil damage exceeded $1,000,000,000 a year. Now whittled down to one sixth that amount, the insect still collects tribute from you, your neighbors, and every other citizen of the nation at the rate of about $1 a year.

Kipling couldn't possibly have had this creature in mind when he made his famous quip about the deadliness of the female. But it is highly appropriate, for the male boll weevil is stolid and comparatively harmless. Dr. W. E. Hinds made careful tests, concluded that the poor fellow doesn't even recognize a member of the opposite sex until she is within about an inch of him. This accounts for the fact that in weevil society, meeting of boy with girl is as accidental as subsequent mating is automatic.

Sexually mature within two to seven days after reaching the adult stage, the female nearly always succeeds in letting some fellow blunder upon her. For more than 99 per cent of all boll weevil eggs are fertile. A single mating probably suffices to fertilize the 120–400 eggs an insect will lay during her life.

She doesn't produce even one, however, without the proper diet. Emerging from hibernation when spring temperatures hover about 64° F., weevils often nibble leaves of early cotton plants. But egg laying doesn't start until females have fed on flower buds. Immature pollen from them is believed to serve as the chemical trigger that sends insects scurrying to begin depositing their eggs for a new generation.

Far from a commonplace act, the boll weevil's egg laying is a precise and delicate operation.

Given freedom of choice, the female selects a blossom bud, or square, that is about six days old. Alighting, she explores to make sure that some other woman didn't beat her to it. Occasionally brushing the surface with her mandibles, she pauses when she reaches a tender spot. Aligning her body with the long axis of the young flower, she takes a firm grip with claws of her forefeet.

Then she bares her teeth—located at the tip of her long snout. Body movement is unnecessary; her head swings freely from the ball-and-socket joint by which it is attached. Slashing through the plant's epidermis, she carefully peels back the coarse outer layer of tissues. Then she quickly eats a deep hole into the square. Reaching the anthers, or pollen sacs, this instinct-guided craftsman enlarges the cavity to flask shape—still eating everything she removes.

With the hole or "puncture" ready, the weevil pivots in a precise half-circle turn. No longer in position to see the shaft just cut, she distends her egg tube so that it presses into the little prepared chamber. Cargo in position, the ovipositor is withdrawn just in time to escape a drop of sticky excrement that serves to seal the puncture against dew, rain, and intruders.

Elliptical when first laid, the colorless egg is so soft that it quickly assumes the shape of the moist haven where it has been deposited. Under optimum conditions, it may hatch in just twenty-four hours; four days is about average for incubation, however.

Pushing out of its shell, the young grub—or larva—is about one twenty-fifth inch in length. It begins eating almost at once. It must gorge constantly in order to survive, for injured cells of the cotton flower frequently begin multiplying at an accelerated rate. Pressure of such proliferation will crush the tender grub unless it eats faster than the plant grows.

After one to three weeks of constant stuffing, during which it has molted two or three times and grown to one fourth inch in length, the legless larva becomes sluggish. So far as cotton is concerned, its deadly work has already been done. Organs of the flower bud have been cut away; it will never bear fruit. Usually it drops to the ground shortly before the grub stops eating.

Having made a glutton of itself on pollen and other vital tissues of the cotton it infests, the larva passes into a dormant or pupal stage. There is no visible activity for a period of five days or so. Inside the translucent mass, however, drastic changes are proceeding.

Nature affords few dramas more vivid and puzzling than

that which marks the end of this stage in the life cycle. At one moment, the pupa has the appearance of a lump of soft soap; there are only faint traces of any individual body parts. Then, in a single quarter hour, eyes form, the characteristic curved snout takes shape, legs and wing covers darken. Given another half hour, the changeling is beginning to move limbs that clearly belong to a boll weevil.

Eight hours later, the fully mature insect crawls through the hole it has cut, just the size of its own body, in order to emerge from the cotton flower where it passed three stages of its life cycle.

This does not, however, mean that bonds with the fiber-producing plant are broken. Far from it. Adult life may be as short as a few weeks or as long as eleven months in the case of successful wintering over. In any case, the insect feeds only upon cotton. Young squares are always preferred, but when they become scarce adult weevils will begin puncturing tough bolls or eating leaves.

Under laboratory conditions, a very few adults have been seen to eat tissues of other plants: okra, hollyhock, hibiscus. There is no known instance of a boll weevil passing its immature stages in any host plant other than those of the genus *Gossypium.*

Once it became clear that weevils are absolutely dependent upon cotton, analysts began to put together some pieces of the puzzle surrounding the sudden rise of a pest that was unknown a few decades ago.

Cotton has been familiar to men since the early days of civilization. A Hindu hymn of the fifteenth century B.C. includes lines suggesting that the vegetable fiber was already being used in weaving. Cultivation spread to Egypt, Arabia, and Persia before the beginning of the present era.

Economic importance to Europeans is another matter; as

late as 1600, cotton was so scarce in England that it was used only for making candlewicks. Expanding trade with India made raw cotton available in quantity. This, in turn, stimulated the mechanical genius of British craftsmen.

Hargreaves' spinning jenny, patented in 1770, opened new doors for cotton. Instead of spinning a single thread by hand, a skilled operator could use the machine to turn out thirty strands simultaneously. Still, such yarn was so soft that it could be used only for the woof in clothmaking. Irish or German linen was needed for the warp. Arkwright's queer new spinning frame solved that problem. Beginning about 1773, machine-made threads could be used for weaving fine, sturdy cloth containing 100 per cent cotton.

Inevitably there was a quick surge in demand. This spurred the Indian trade—but seamen couldn't bring enough to satisfy needs of a fast-developing cloth industry. Something would have to be done to increase the world supply of this exciting stuff. Eyes of Europeans naturally turned across the Atlantic.

For years it had been known that the New World included native cottons. We now know that it was important in the economy of pre-Incan tribesmen of Peru, familiar in several sections of Brazil and Central America. Aztecs of Mexico collected cotton blankets as part of their tribute from subject peoples.

But in the seventeenth century, Europeans had no acquaintance with these matters. They simply knew that Columbus found cotton in the Bahama Islands, the Spanish had fostered cultivation in some of their colonies, and scattered plots of it were being grown along the North American seaboard.

Actually it was planted along rivers of Virginia as early as 1619. But administrators didn't encourage such ventures. England was much more interested in tobacco, Indian corn, and lumber. Bounties were offered to encourage the planting of mulberry trees and the raising of silk, then considered to be the fiber of the future. Savannah, Georgia, was chosen as the site of a reeling plant; for a time silk farmers harvested some 10,000 pounds of cocoons each year.

About 800 pounds of cotton were bagged in the Carolinas and forwarded to Liverpool in 1764. Textile leaders of England were mildly excited, for their mills were using 4,000,000 pounds of cotton each year. Much of their supply came from the British West Indies, though substantial quantities were brought from India and from Spanish colonies in the New World. Perhaps the farms of North America could produce more and cheaper cotton . . .

No one recognized what was happening, but converging forces were beginning to form a vast ecological spark gap. Demand for cotton, with a host of economic and industrial aspects, constituted one pole in the field of tension. The biological versatility of plants and insects, plus America's great stretches of uncultivated land, made up the other. Soon the poles would be adjusted so precisely that it would require no effort for the boll weevil to jump the gap.

First, however, a major technical advance was necessary. Men now had an established market for cotton goods, plus adequate machinery with which to transform lint into finished cloth. But the supply of fiber was strictly limited by the slow and tedious task of picking strands of cotton from the seed to which they are attached.

Eli Whitney didn't know that by solving this problem he took the last step to guarantee the rise of the boll weevil.

Once the gin went into action, U.S. cotton production soared. England imported nearly half a million pounds in 1793, the first year Whitney's machine was in general use. Twelve months later, the figure soared to three times that total. In 1800, nearly 18,000,000 pounds crossed the Atlantic. By 1818, North America was producing some 95,000,000 pounds of cotton each year for domestic use and export.

Complex feedback processes moved faster and faster. The increased production of cotton spurred the invention of new and bigger machinery to handle it from the time it left the picker's bag until it became a finished garment. In turn, availability of a huge textile industry stimulated farmers to abandon other crops in favor of the fiber with a guaranteed market.

In the climatic zone favorable to cotton, fields grew bigger and closer together. Pioneers moved West, taking bags of seed with them. Pushing across a great belt in the South, cotton plantations fostered the expansion of slavery—for cheap labor was required for cultivation and harvesting. Jumping the Mississippi, this elaborate complex spurted forward with new vigor in the wonderfully fertile regions that then constituted the southwestern frontier.

Turn back to 1764 just long enough to remember that the year's crop yielded 800 pounds for export. Just a century and a quarter later, the U.S. cotton belt was spewing out 6,094,000,000 pounds of cotton each season. A textile expert dissected that figure, announced that it meant enough fiber to make thirty-four feet of good calico for every person in the world.

Two years later, a few specimens of the still-obscure *Anthonomus grandis* crossed the Rio Grande. Under favorable circumstances the full egg-to-egg life cycle can be accomplished in about three weeks. Much of the cotton belt has five months of warm weather. That means a potential of seven generations in a single season. Theoretically, every pair of winged invaders could have some 12,000,000 descendants before the end of their first year in residence.

In practice, no species ever reaches theoretical levels of multiplication. Still, entomologists later concluded that under actual conditions when no poison is used on cotton, a hardy egg-laden female weevil can live to see about 2,000,000 progeny join her in puncturing squares and bolls.

Had they made a deliberate effort, farmers couldn't have prepared a region more suited to rapid build-up of insect population. *Anthonomus* was probably linked with wild tree cotton in Central America many centuries ago. Even under crude cultivation, plants were scattered about in small fields. Many native varieties have a short fruiting season, and few primitive planters had rows in which all the cotton ran true to one type.

As opposed to scattered and varied plants with blossoms available only a few weeks, U.S. mass producers of cotton had prepared concentrated fields of uniform plants whose fruiting season extended over a period of months. Furthermore, this vast seedbed of opportunity offered the boll weevil a haven from which native insect enemies were missing.

Under these circumstances, a debacle was inevitable.

During the sixty years that have ensued since men first began to feel the effects of weevil attack, there have followed three separate sets of adjustments.

First, scientists launched a counteroffensive. A single federal agency has spent $3,500,000 in research; many other state and private organizations have tried to find ways to control the cotton foe. Poisoning has proved the most effective single expedient, though it is all but futile unless combined with suitable cultural practices.

Very early there were determined efforts to enlist the aid of insects that prey on boll weevils. No such program has yet proved of importance. Kelep ants greatly reduce damage to cotton in Guatemala by preying on weevils; brought to this country, the ants failed to thrive. Other predators and parasites imported from Peru and Kenya Colony also failed to become established.

Neither has there been success in the attempt to breed a variety of cotton that will be tough enough to resist the insect's tiny teeth. Plants that mature early are now generally favored, for damage mounts during late summer. All man's efforts have brought about no more than 40 per cent reduction from the period of peak losses.

Natural forces have been operating, however, to foster a second set of adjustments. For the blowup of the weevil population soon led numerous native insects to make changes in their diet. Some have simply added the boll weevil to the list of those they attack; others have made it a staple item of food.

At least twelve types of ants now prey on immature forms of the cotton insect. Where such ants are especially numerous, they may kill half the larvae that are hatched. Over the cotton belt as a whole, they probably thin weevil ranks by about 16 per cent each year.

More than two dozen insects have become parasitic upon the newcomer from Mexico; together, these species account for millions of weevil casualties in each square mile of cotton. Where parasites are scarce, they help the farmer but little. In areas where they abound, they may kill 77 per cent of all weevils.

Most or all native insect-eating birds will feed on weevils. When they begin to emerge from hibernation in the spring, they are attacked by wrens, titmice, blackbirds, meadow larks, and other less familiar species such as the pipit. There is no way to estimate the total effect of bird activity—but it is believed much less significant than that of predatory and parasitic insects. Though man did nothing to bring them about, the combined influence of these converging forces is probably greater than that of all the scientific discoveries that help protect cotton from weevils.

Just as the insect's rise to prominence required an elaborate pattern of contributing factors, so its onslaughts have affected areas of human life far removed from the cotton field. These constitute the third set of adjustments that have followed in the wake of the struggle of weevil against man.

In a very real sense, boll weevils helped launch the current social revolution taking place in the U.S. South. For crop losses forced the abandonment of tenancy as the prevailing pattern. Men quit trying to cultivate worn-out land, moved to town, and formed labor pools to attract industry into Dixie. Hedging against losses from weevils helped accelerate crop diversification and the swing toward raising of beef cattle.

After the initial shock of hysteria had passed, citizens of Enterprise, Alabama, concluded that the weevil invasion had been a good thing. So a few years ago they erected a town marker expressing their gratitude that the insect made them give up a static one-crop economy.

Any attempt to enumerate or assess all factors linked with the rise and spread of the boll weevil is doomed to failure. At most we can conclude that it provides the most elaborate of modern case histories illustrating the basic principle that when man changes any aspect of a biological pattern, vast and unexpected results may ensue.

Big Bruin: Half Brother in a Shaggy Coat

Peesunt tossed her head. "Sing if you wish," she told her two companions. "But I shall not. This year, the huckleberries are fat. While you are trying to please the bears, I shall be filling my basket."

She gathered so many berries that on the way home her pack strap broke. Still singing, her friends left Peesunt behind in the twilight. As she worked to mend the strap, voices of two young men came to her out of the gloom. They offered to carry her load, so she accepted and fell in step with them. Not until they were well along a strange trail did the maiden notice they wore bear robes.

Led to a big shelter, she found the campfire surrounded by men and women clad in skins. Peesunt sat down to eat with them. No words were spoken until White Mouse tugged at the maiden's robe—now coated with the long gray hairs of a grizzly bear—and gently explained:

"Granddaughter, when you did not sing, the bears came to see why you were silent. They liked your comeliness and have brought you to their lodge. You shall take the son of the bear chief as your mate, and shall be mother of his children."

In time, says the folklore of American tribesmen, the Indian maiden gave birth to twins—half human, half bear. They became cunning hunters and mighty warriors whose exploits are commemorated in ritual, songs, and carvings on totem poles.

Closely related versions of the bear-mother motif have been prominent in the religion of many primitive peoples widely separated in place and time. From Ainu lore of ancient Japan to Tlingit tales of Alaska, from Scandinavian sagas to Russian and Greek mythology, there runs the weirdly recurrent theme: human blood flows through the veins of many a shaggy-coated warrior who has the head of a bear but who walks like a man.

Viewed from the perspective of geological epochs rather than human generations, this idea is strangely suggestive. For members of the bear family have more man-like traits than any other widespread competitors of the queer hairless beast who in recent times has come to rule the earth.

Comparatively soon after the age of reptiles faded into the epoch dominated by mammals, ancestors of the bear began to thrive. Fossil remains of the first true bears date from the Miocene age.

Racial differences make the modern polar bear as distinct from the grizzly as are Africa's pygmy tribesmen from big blond Vikings. Yet all bears share a number of traits that set them apart from other creatures—and contribute to their capacity to meet human competition.

Unlike cats and most dogs, all bears have five digits on each foot. Many creatures can withdraw their talons at will; claws of bears and nails of men are fixed in position. Many animals walk gracefully upon their toes; bears and men throw their weight squarely upon the soles of their feet—so lumber along comparatively clumsily. Bear tracks are remarkably similar to human footprints. It is this feature, say some naturalists, that contributes to the legend of the "abominable snowman." Giant man-like tracks in the snow of Himalayan peaks probably come from the feet of red bears—not from a strange race of fur-covered men living on 20,000-foot peaks.

Like *Homo sapiens,* members of the family *Ursus* have rounded ears that are permanently erect. And man's complete lack of a tail is just a trifle more radical than the state of a nine-foot grizzly equipped with a three-inch stump.

Capacity to walk upright upon hind legs—and even to dance clumsily in that position—dramatizes bruin's resemblance to man. Many creatures produce young that are ready to fend for themselves soon after birth; human babies and bear cubs are helpless for comparatively long periods. Born blind and toothless, the cub of a black bear weighs only four pounds after forty days.

Bruin differs widely from his human rival at one point, however. Mating occurs only once in two years—and the season is limited to three or four weeks. This factor is undoubtedly linked with the failure of bears to develop a cosmetic industry, motion pictures, or syndicated columns.

Actually, the typical bear is so preoccupied with eating that he has time for only a brief and occasional interest in sex. Many animals restrict their diet to a narrow list; bears feed on a range of substances wider than that of any other creatures—with the possible exception of night club habitués.

Bruin is the largest land carnivore of recent geological epochs; his remote ancestors probably ate nothing but flesh. Through a little-understood series of changes and adaptations, both his body and his appetite have been modified. Hence bears thrive in regions where insistence upon a meat diet would lead to extinction.

Teeth of most bears are startlingly different from those of such flesheaters as the lion and tiger. Canines and incisors are sharp enough to bite and tear through tough muscle; a hungry grizzly is one of the most dangerous creatures on the planet. Major riddles center around the bear's molars, however. For instead of having flesh-cutting surfaces like those of typical carnivores, bruin's are broad and tuberculated. This means that he has the proper apparatus to grind vegetable substances—and hence can feed on almost anything living.

Just what factors influenced the age-long process by which bears became equipped with so queer an assortment of eating tools, no one knows precisely.

Present-day grizzlies and polar bears are chiefly carnivorous; nearly all other bears feed largely or entirely on vegetables and insects. Fruits, berries, and nuts are considered delicacies; the American black bear sometimes breaks down twenty-foot scrub oaks for the sheer delight of stuffing himself on acorns. He also relishes everything from bitter cherries to skunk cabbage. The stomach of one specimen killed by a hunter was examined and found to include two quarts of yellow jackets—swallowed whole.

Most bears enjoy birds' eggs, fish, grubs, and small game. When very hungry, any of the larger types will kill elk, moose, and deer. But even in regions where lambs and calves are to be had for the taking, a brown bear will usually pass them in preference to a field of standing corn. Even after reaching 1600 pounds, the Kodiak will graze like a cow.

Bruin's love for a queer substance which bees store in hollow trees is proverbial. Few wild creatures consider it worth the taking; bears will endure any number of attacks in order to rob a hive. It may have been a brown-clad thief high in a tree who first attracted man's attention to honey. At any rate, the sticky stuff came to be highly prized and was the only sweet used during most of human history.

Like medieval barons, male bears pay little attention to their progeny—and probably do not so much as recognize them. With she-bears it is a different story. Cubs remain with their mothers for eighteen months or more. During much of the time, they are in nursery school—with the mother actively teaching them how to climb trees, scoop fish from streams, and stalk small game. Veteran outdoorsmen vow that, in the Pacific Northwest, orphan bears never quite master the art of catching salmon with the skill of those taught by their mothers.

Small wonder that men of ancient and primitive races, divided on many issues, were united in their admiration for the animal foe so strangely human in structure and ways.

Plains Indians who succeeded in killing a grizzly counted it a coup in the same fashion that they recorded victory over a hostile warrior. Aboriginal tribesmen of Japan made the festival of the bear a high point of their worship—and honored great men by comparing them to the animal. Among the early Norsemen the bear-like hero, Berserk, was so venerated that his name became frozen in language. Even today, one who fights with the blind fury of a wounded bear-man is said to *go berserk*.

Artemis, a principal goddess in Greek mythology, was for centuries a central figure in bear cults. Ancient rites in the land of Socrates included dances by groups of young girls wearing bearskins—perpetuating dim traces of earlier ceremonies in which Artemis herself was a bear to whom human sacrifice was offered.

Even that favorite of children in the TV age, "Goldilocks and the Three Bears," is probably a modernized version of ancient tales similar to that in which Peesunt figures. For in many an old legend, a maiden becomes enamored of some shaggy male and takes up residence in the house of the bears.

Long regarded as pure fantasy, these yarns are relics from one of the most vivid chapters in the story of mankind. For during that long and rather vaguely defined period in which the cave man came into prominence, humans and bears not only lived under the same roofs—they fought fiercely for possession of the only existing shelters.

Ursus spelaeus, the bear that inhabited caverns, flourished an estimated 70,000 years ago. At least in Spain, scattered colonies of the big animals survived until geology's "day before yesterday"—that period, some 20,000 years ago, when *Homo sapiens* wholly superseded Neanderthal man.

From the study of skeletons, it is believed that the cave bear must have weighed 1200–1500 pounds. Reared upon hind legs, waving tremendous paws, and snarling from a bulldog-shaped mouth, the beast must have been the most fearful foe any Stone Age householder could encounter in a dark corridor leading off the family cavern. Though it killed woolly rhinoceros, wild ox, and mammoth, badly worn molars of fossil skulls suggest that the cave bear ate considerable vegetable matter.

Much evidence indicates that these animals wintered in European caves long before man began to use them. Hence it is not improbable that bears may have stimulated some Neanderthal genius to conceive the idea that life would be easier and safer with a cavern as a place of shelter.

This first and crudest of human habitations was not easily won; chipped stone weapons, alone, hardly gave man the means to best so powerful an animal. Fire may have been the key to human victory; smoked out of his lair while groggy from winter sleep, a giant bear was still a fearful foe for men armed only with the *coup de poing,* or hand hatchet.

Warm interglacial periods with long summers and abundant food were favorable to the cave bear. It was climatic change, rather than strength or skill of man, that led to the downfall of the beast. Long periods of intense cold reduced the supply of food and extended the duration of the winter sleep. Consequently, bears began to develop bone diseases —especially in the breastbone and vertebrae—now common to their descendants that are kept in zoos.

At some time shortly before or after the end of the last great Ice Age, ranks of the cave bear became suddenly thin. Human remains from the cave of Le Moustier indicate that men bore the cold and damp in better fashion than their furry competitors. But in addition to isolated pockets of surviving cave bears, humans of the epoch were threatened with a new menace: rise of the brown bear.

Still found throughout much of Europe, the beast posed a daily menace to the queer creature then emerging into true manhood. Bones of brown bears have been found in startling numbers in most major caves of France, Germany, Belgium, England, Italy, Poland, the Balkans, and southern Russia. It was this bruin—literally "the brown one"—that figured so prominently in pre-historic European art and religion.

Recognition of this fact has come very recently, however, as a strange aftermath of human warfare. Slaughter of cattle during World War I produced so great a shortage of animals that farmers were stimulated into a frenzied search for a new source of fertilizer. It was found in the guano of caves—centuries-old accumulations of bat droppings. Commercial excavation spurred the study of caverns and brought new understanding of both humans and bears who inhabited them long ago.

By the time pre-historic man developed artistic skill, he was competing with the brown bear rather than the earlier and bigger cave bear. In the caverns of France alone, modern diggers have found remnants of more than 3000 drawings and paintings. Reindeer and horses figure prominently in many of them; the wild ox, woolly rhinoceros, and mammoth are less common. There are many representations of the bear —none of the dog or any member of the cat family.

A noted French cavern yielded an unbaked clay figure—a bear nearly four feet long, the figure mutilated by dart thrusts and hinting darkly of the pre-historic hunter's magic. Not many miles away, another cave includes a gallery with a magnificent mural figure of a bear—along with representations of men followed by women with pendant breasts.

In Switzerland, the cavern of Drachenloch must have served as a primitive temple. In it was found a crude altar piled high with the skulls of bears. All surviving traces of bear worship, plus the legendary mating of bears and humans, point dimly toward the period when survival of the race demanded that men gain mastery over bears.

Though man's superior brain proved more significant than the greater brawn of his foe, the age-long struggle is not over. Human victory has not meant extinction, or even near extinction, as in the case of the buffalo. Rather, bears are still co-inhabitants of two thirds of the planet's temperate-zone land surface. Like men, existing types are divided into a number of distinct racial groups.

Permanently adapted to a narrow environment, polar bears are the most specialized of modern species. Though their white fur is tinged with yellow from long immersion in brine, it blends naturally into snowy backgrounds. So the bear stalking his prey is practically invisible—only his black nose is easily spied, and he sometimes covers it with his tongue as he lurks in hiding.

Soles of the polar bear's feet are covered with close-set hairs that enable him to walk securely on ice. There is a bit of webbing between his toes, adding to his equipment for long-distance swimming. Animals have been seen sixty miles from land, still going strong. Nose, ears, and eyes are so arranged that they protrude naturally when all the rest of the body is submerged. A third eyelid, nearly transparent, serves as a filter to protect the eyes from the glare of the polar sun.

In a time of stress, these animals will eat grass and other vegetable matter—even seaweed. But their staple is meat: seals, walrus, foxes, caribou, birds, and shellfish. From constant feeding on sea creatures, the polar bear's liver is so rich that three ounces will yield enough vitamin A to supply a man for twelve months.

When food is plentiful, the polar bear is not likely to attack humans unless they venture very close. During winter, however, a big animal will track men across the ice just as it stalks any other game.

Veteran trainer William Hagenbeck branded the white giant as the most difficult to handle of any animal ever exhibited. After trying to train seventy members of the species, he declared that only two of them seemed to enjoy their work!

It was their savage disposition that prevented bears from becoming the first domestic animals. For tens of thousands of years, they were more intimately associated with man than any other beast—yet resisted taming. Comparatively soon after early dogs became numerous, they joined forces with humans. Once he gained canine partners, pre-historic man was better equipped to take the offensive against bear rivals.

Among polar bears, resistance to living in a man-shaped environment goes so far that it is difficult to bring up young ones in captivity. Most mothers kept in zoos neglect their babies so badly that they die. Sultana, a big female seen by more than 25,000,000 visitors to Milwaukee's zoo, was the first polar bear to rear cubs in confinement. Captured at the age of one year, she lived to be thirty-five, gave birth to twelve cubs and reared eleven of them.

Most brown and black bears are more docile than their cousins from the Arctic. They differ in size and details of anatomy as well as coloring. Yet the lines of separation are not too broad for interbreeding. At the National Zoo in Washington, a brown bear persuaded to mate with a polar bear gave birth to strong cubs.

Scotland's last brown bear was killed in 1057, and the animal soon became extinct in England. There are many surviving groups in Europe and Asia, however. America's closely related common black bear is in no danger of extinction; numbers are actually increasing in regions as thickly settled as Pennsylvania.

Ursus horribilis, "the terrible bear" or grizzly, has not fared so well. During pioneer days, this beast was undisputed master of the whole U.S. Northwest. Three times as big as a lion, a grizzly can break the back of an elk with one blow. Far more dependent upon meat than his smaller brown and black cousins, the grizzly now thrives only in remote mountainous regions and national parks.

Other members of the family, distinguished by special bodily features and ways of life, are found in many regions. Of them all, the sloth bear is perhaps the most bizarre. Abundant in the mountains of India, the shaggy fellow lacks one pair of upper front teeth. His cheek teeth are unusually small, while his lips and tongue are long and mobile. Nostrils are equipped with a set of special valves.

All this equipment is admirably suited to his special appetite. For though he eats fruits and honey, his staple food is white ants. After scratching off the top of a termite mound, the bear applies his mouth to the hole and sucks so strongly that he pulls insects from a considerable depth.

Known to modern city dwellers only as a curiosity in the zoo and a figure in fables for the children, bears of all types are so overshadowed by rifle-bearing men that there is no longer any serious competition between the two families. But the period of bitter struggle was many times as long as the recent era of human dominance. Given a few more biological advantages, the beast who seems almost a crude copy of man might have exterminated his hairless competitor.

Gadus morrhua:
The Fish That Made History

Blue whales, killer sharks, giant squid, and their exotic fellows have played central parts in many an adventure tale. *Gadus morrhua,* the common cod, seldom figures in a yarn of danger and heroism. But to an extent greater than that of any other creature of the sea, this soft-finned denizen of northern waters has shaped the course of history.

Captain John Smith, fresh from a voyage of exploration along the New England coast, grew positively rapturous as he described the "pretty sport" of pulling up two or three hundred cod in a day. "Honorable and worthy countrymen," he urged, "let not the meanness of the word *fish* distaste you, for it will afford as good gold as the mines of Guiana, with less hazard and charge, and more certainty and facility."

Most folk at the court of James I succeeded in restraining their enthusiasm. This barren land of which Smith and his comrades prattled did not deserve a name so fair as that of New England. It had no gold, silk, spices, or wool. Only rude savages roamed its rocky shores. Religious malcontents might eye it as a possible place of refuge, but diplomats were too busy with important matters to give it more than passing notice.

So the Pilgrims who settled Plymouth in 1620 didn't bother with the formality of getting a royal charter. They governed themselves under the Mayflower Compact until absorbed by the Massachusetts Bay Colony in 1691. By then, England's rulers were beginning to realize that in finding an exile, the sturdy Pilgrims had stumbled upon something big.

There are persistent tales that cod saved some pioneer settlers from starvation. Soon fishing passed from an emergency device to a fast-growing industry. The Old World constituted a colossal market, ready to exchange precious metals and manufactured goods for dried cod. So the first product exported from Massachusetts was a cargo of fish.

By 1634, an early merchant prince had a fleet of eight vessels at Marblehead. Twelve months later, Portsmouth alone boasted six big fishing shallops, five smaller boats, and thirteen skiffs. Governor Winthrop solemnly recorded that just a generation after the colony was established as a tiny, wavering beachhead on a hostile continent, one season saw 300,000 dry fish shipped to market.

World demand for cod was at a level seldom attained by any commodity. According to an early description, its flesh was recognized to be "different from other fishes like the salmon and herring: rich and gelatinous without being fatty." Sun-dried or cured by salting, it kept indefinitely under almost any conditions.

Remember that this was still the epoch B.T.C.—Before Tin Cans. Ships going below the line could take only a few food items. Many staples that resisted rot were likely to yield to attacks of mold or maggots. Lacking the tough fish that was known as "beef of the sea," many a long equatorial voyage would have been impossible. Cod was also in great demand by soldiers, planters in tropical lands, and the pious of Catholic Europe. Small wonder that fish became to New England what wool was to Britain and coffee is to Brazil.

Rapidly pushing out from coastal waters, seamen from the colonies challenged European powers for control of the greatest codfishing region on earth—the Grand Banks off Newfoundland. Wealth and skill gained in the trade boosted the growth of a colonial merchant marine. Young ports like Salem, Bristol, and Boston began to vie with old ones of Spain, France, and England.

Small wonder that the cod made indelible impressions upon New England. It appeared on the corporate seal of the Plymouth Land Company prior to 1661. Many legal seals, including those central in witchcraft trials, bore the codfish emblem. A carved replica of the fish still has a place of honor in the Massachusetts State House, and the cod was long depicted upon coins, bank notes, and revenue stamps of the colony.

Familiar in waters of northern Europe since very early times, the cod soared to global prominence after Cabot discovered North America. Waters off Iceland had supplied most of Europe's salt fish; now the center shifted far to the West. Long before anyone thought of establishing colonies in New England, fleets from European ports began making the long voyage to fishing grounds not far from Canada.

Portugal and France led the movement. Both nations were weak in agricultural power—but had plenty of salt with which to cure fish. So when Jacques Cartier made his voyage of 1536, he found his countrymen already established as fishermen on the island of St. Pierre. With its companion, Miquelon, the tiny bit of land just south of Newfoundland comprises the oldest of French colonies.

England was not yet competing for mastery of the region.

She had no navy of importance, and her commercial vessels were greatly outnumbered by those of her rivals. Though it required a six months' voyage to fill the hold with cod, French, Portuguese, and Dutch ships of 50 to 250 tons rushed to enter the Grand Banks trade. One seaman estimated that in 1630 there were 300 French vessels scrambling for wealth from these "silver mines of the sea." With their rivals, he noted, they brought home countless tons of cod "wherewith they feed nearly all Europe and supply all sea-going vessels."

Lack of enthusiasm on the part of political leaders did not deter Britain's fishermen. Some of them entered the scramble for the new cod banks about 1600. Fleets from Bristol and Devon multiplied so rapidly that soon they could supply the home market and have an excess for export. Their activities were complicated by the need for cheap salt, produced in Mediterranean regions by the evaporation of sea water. Demand for fish and for salt created a need for more seagoing vessels and crews to man them.

So the shipping industry of Britain expanded in several directions at once. Pre-occupied with the gold of South America, Spain neglected other interests. English ships began making direct voyages from the fishing grounds of the North Atlantic to the ports of cod-hungry southern Europe. By 1634, an estimated 18,680 British tars were engaged in the Newfoundland fishery. They not only brought gold to England; their fleets gave ideal training to men destined to sail armed vessels of the expanding Royal Navy.

It is not possible to measure the extent to which her interest in the cod contributed to the sudden rise of England as an ocean power. Too many other factors were involved to warrant an estimate of the precise influence of New World fishing. But it was a potent element in the build-up of ships and sailors in numbers sufficient to challenge the supremacy of Spain.

Many who fought under Sir Francis Drake gained their sea legs in the cod trade; after the defeat of the Armada in 1588, England won a near monopoly in this most important of all food fishes. She held it some fifty years, then lost out to New England ports that had the advantage of proximity to the Banks.

Having boosted both Britain and her colonies to new power, Atlantic fishing grounds loomed to major importance about conference tables. John Adams represented New England in final peace negotiations after the War of Independence. He received a barrage of letters from regions as distant as North Carolina, urging that he hold out for title to the cod regions.

One such plea suggested that "the fishery of Newfoundland appears to be a mine of infinitely greater value than Mexico or Peru." Adams agreed with that judgment, noting that cod were already being exchanged for the gold and silver of Europe plus the rum and molasses of the West Indies. In addition, said Adams, "the fisheries have been the nursery of seamen and source of naval power, indispensably necessary to the accomplishment and the preservation of our independence."

While statesmen solemnly discussed treaties in which it figured, scientists investigated the life history and habits of the cod. A member of the genus *Gadus*, one of its most remarkable features is its set of unsymmetrical fins—three along the back and two under the belly. Its tail, suggest some specialists, is a clue to the cod's rather sluggish disposition. Many creatures have divided tails thought to be adapted for fast swimming because capable of swishing about without interfering with the slip stream from the fish's body.

Guided by its nearly square tail, the cod moves leisurely. Fishermen frequently label it "stupid," because it is so easily mastered. Even when hooked only through its rubbery lip, a sixty-pound specimen is likely to yield without a struggle.

Present-day steamers equipped with big nets catch multitudes of cod before they reach maturity. So the majority entering commerce range from about ten to thirty pounds. One patriarch caught in 1895 was more than six feet long, weighed 211½ pounds.

Formerly far more abundant than they are today, big cod have yielded some of the sea's oddest prizes. A bunch of keys was found in the stomach of one, while others have contained such gear as a long piece of tallow candle, a white turnip, a partridge, and a heavy book bound in calfskin. Glass and stones are found in many specimens; a few rare fishes and shells would not be known to exist had they not been discovered in the stomachs of captured cod.

Like many other bony fishes, the cod has strong teeth with which it seizes and sometimes tears its prey. Mollusks, crustaceans, and small fishes are usually swallowed whole; six dogfish averaging nine inches in length were found in the stomach of a single cod. Digestive juices are so potent that bones and shells present no problem; after brief soaking in the gullet of its big foe, a crab becomes so soft that its legs may be twisted around one's finger.

Lacking familiarity with mature specimens, one familiar with early stages in the life cycle would consider the cod to be among the most vulnerable of all creatures. In many waters, spawning females may be taken over a period of three to four months. Frequently an individual is so ripe that clear eggs will run from her body without application of pressure.

Eggs released into the sea are so tiny that nineteen of them laid side to side will stretch just one inch. Because they are lighter than water, transparent ova float on or near the surface—not haphazardly, but according to a precise pattern. Each minute egg hangs in such fashion that its micropyle, or aperture for admission of the fertilizing male cell, is turned downward. Males encounter bobbing clusters of eggs which somehow trigger reactions in the milt glands. Streams of spermatozoa are released into the water; swimming upward, each has a chance of reaching and entering a waiting egg.

After about twelve days of development, the mature embryo pierces the egg capsule with its tail and emerges into the sea tail first. About one sixth of an inch in length, the codling still has with it a store of unused yolk from the egg. At once, it begins feeding upon organisms smaller than itself. For two or three months, however, it remains so fragile that it is transparent—and colorless except for blue-black eyes and a few minute spots on body and head.

Preyed upon by hosts of enemies, an occasional codling chances to survive. Sometimes it is saved by one of the queerest of all shelters—the blue jellyfish. This huge creature, which may measure six feet across, is death to many kinds of sea life coming in reach of its tentacles. Yet the big killer acts as a kind of citadel under which tiny fishes may retreat without being molested.

Neither this nor any other haven gives great life expectancy to young cod, however. One of the few aspects of the fish's natural history that has entered general knowledge is its prodigious fertility. Typical twenty-pound specimens produce more than 2,000,000 eggs each season. David Starr Jordan once estimated that if all progeny of a single cod should survive and grow to maturity, they would fill the entire Atlantic with a solid mass of fish!

Such speculation may be a pleasant way to indulge one's fancy briefly, but is far removed from biological reality. Actually, codlings face so many dangers that survival is weirdly rare. Out of each million eggs, perhaps a single fish may live to be caught in a net and used as human food. Even then, life usually ends years before the maximum span is reached.

The application of industrial techniques to fishing has actually threatened the future of the species. As late as 1883, it didn't seem possible that man's activities could ever affect the prolific cod. Thomas H. Huxley advanced that view in the address with which he opened the International Fishery Exhibition. The development of steam trawling later showed that the organic wealth of the seas is by no means inexhaustible. So cod were the first ocean creatures to be hatched artificially, released in huge numbers in attempts to preserve the world supply.

Well over 2,000,000,000 pounds of cod now enter commerce each year. No one has sufficient information to hazard an estimate as to the total catch during the past four centuries. But this special source of food clearly played a major role in the modern period of expanding civilization.

Literally millions of cod went down the gullets of explorers, adventurers, seamen, and soldiers. Casks of salt fish were packed into the interior of South America by mule train. Whole fleets laden with sun-dried cod helped provision European cities whose population was increasing faster than food supplies. As a cheap source of protein that would keep indefinitely even in the tropics, the cod was a small but real supporting factor in the development of a slave culture in the West Indies.

Among biological side effects was the contribution to the extinction of an unrelated species. Unable to bring meat from Europe to the Grand Banks, many sailing vessels depended upon the great auk as a major source of bait for their hooks. On the way to cod waters, ship after ship stopped to permit the crew to feast and fill bait barrels. Continuing for more than two centuries, unrestricted raids upon the auk led to its disappearance about 1844.

Still another repercussion was in an unexpected aspect of human health. Very early, tough fishermen who patched their weather-beaten cheeks with tar developed a practice of saving nearly every part of the cod. Though the split bodies were of most importance, few parts were discarded.

Tongues, long cut out at the moment of capture and strung on wires to afford a tally of each fisherman's daily catch, were salted in barrels. Air bladders, or sounds, were important in the isinglass trade. Cod cheeks were used for the crew's midnight "soup of sorrow"—so called because the man who once tasted it could expect to spend his life on the Banks. Skin was salvaged for the glue trade. Livers were thrown into barrels and permitted to rot, yielding several grades of oil useful in tanning and in the manufacture of soap.

As the tempo of the industry was accelerated, cod-liver oil became a standard item of commerce—for a hogshead of the heavy stuff is a by-product of each four or five tons of fish. Fishermen used the oil as a poultice for wounds; at least as early as 1770, uneducated folk of North Atlantic ports were experimenting with it as a food supplement for the sick and aged.

After 1820, numerous physicians of Holland and France employed cod-liver oil in the treatment of rickets—the comparatively new malady that was affecting more and more children reared in cities. Increasing concern with scientific medicine led to a repudiation of folk remedies. Fish oil was challenged along with herb teas and the like.

It remained in use as a general tonic, but not until E. V. McCollum proved its merits in 1921 did cod-liver oil win recognition as a specific cure for rickets. Later study showed its action to be due to vitamin factors; on the basis of understanding won from the study of "sunlight of the sea," other treatments were developed with such effectiveness that rickets can now be fully controlled.

Neither the fish nor its by-product is so vital in contemporary life as in the past. New laboratory processes have about made the oil obsolete in medicine, and advances in agriculture have yielded fresh sources of cheap protein. Today we could undoubtedly make adjustments if the cod were to disappear completely. Lacking four centuries of its influence, whether we would be where we are in the development of North America and in the world balance of political power is quite a different question.

Br'er Rabbit's Biological Blitz

Thomas Austin meant no harm. He simply wanted to play the part of an English country squire. It would make the Australian bush a bit more like Yorkshire, he reasoned, if he could invite his neighbors over for a real old-time rabbit hunt. So he instructed his agent back home to send him two dozen animals for breeding stock.

Rabbits were no strangers to the land of kangaroos and gum trees. Early in their race to colonize new lands, Europeans had discovered that bunnies surpass all other livestock in ability to survive long voyages. Many a desolate island was therefore stocked with them, so that descendants would be on hand to provide meat for shipwrecked sailors.

Old records indicate that a few rabbits accompanied the first settlers to arrive Down Under in 1788. They were domestic breeds that provided choice meat for the table, but lacked the vigor that made their wild cousins fit animals for the chase. So for his estate near Melbourne, Squire Austin specified that he wanted the common European rabbit, rather than its tame descendants.

Late in 1859, his animals arrived on the clipper ship *Light-*

ning. Had folk only known it, the name of the vessel was symbolic. For the rabbits it brought to Australia generated a bolt of biological lightning that seared half the continent.

Liberated in Barone Park, the immigrants from cold, fox-filled England found things very much to their liking: plenty of sweet grass, no animal foes to prey on them, and a climate just right for year-round breeding. So all twelve bucks settled down to the serious business of rearing a family. They succeeded so well that during the next six years, Austin shot and trapped nearly 20,000 rabbits—and estimated that at least 10,000 survived at the end of the period.

By 1866, descendants of the settler's game stock were fanning out into the whole Geelong district of Southeast Australia. During the next half century, their progeny became the most notorious animal pests of modern times—with major impact upon the productivity of more than 1,000,000,000 acres of land.

Attempts at control began very early. It would be a simple matter, authorities reasoned, to trap or shoot enough animals to thin their ranks. So a one-shilling bounty was offered for rabbit tails. Though taxpayers grumbled at the bureaucratic waste involved, governmental agencies began planning to build long stretches of rabbitproof fences.

In the single decade 1880–89, departments of the Victorian government paid £350,000 for rabbit tails and wire fences. South Australia and New South Wales poured four times as much into the struggle. Bunnies took the attack calmly, kept on bringing one litter after another. It was nature's power of survival versus human ingenuity—a fight to the finish, with no holds barred.

Though man's optimism never died, it was clear from the beginning that rabbits have major advantages.

Reproductive capacity is first on the list. Under favorable

circumstances, a doe may drop as many as six litters a year —with an average of six in each. Human babies require 180 days to double their weight at birth; bunnies pull the trick in less than a week. After ten to fourteen days, they leave the warren and begin to fare for themselves; in four months they are parents with their own brood to feed.

Theoretically, in just three years the descendants of a single pair could multiply to 13,000,000. Field conditions never permit survival of more than a limited per cent; Australia proved strangely suited for increasing the life expectancy of rabbits. Thomas Austin's animals spawned a brood that during fifty years was target for every lethal device man could conceive; yet rabbit population soared to an estimated 2,000,000,000—about three hundred times the human population of the Pacific continent.

Especially in good sheep country, the diet of the hopping animals gives them a jump on competitors. According to one English specialist, rabbits have never been known to eat laurel. If that is true, it is the only plant valued by man that is safe from the chisel-like teeth of Peter and his cousins.

Rabbits are fond of succulent plants like alfalfa, clover, corn, and cabbage. They revel in the sweet grasses of fine pasture country. But they also thrive on everything from oak seedlings to prickly pear. Given a free hand in grazing regions, they select the best grasses—and nibble plants so low that they die.

Veteran ranchers vow that during favorable seasons, rabbits eat practically around the clock. Summer or winter, any nine of them will consume enough forage to sustain two fine sheep. Since wool is basic to Australia's economy, settlers vowed they'd soon rid the continent of its four-legged invaders.

Shooting and trapping didn't quite do the trick. Conditions

were so favorable that new bunnies arrived faster than their brothers and sisters could be dispatched. In order to turn the tide, reasoned experts, it would be necessary to introduce to Australia one or more natural enemies of the rabbit.

Logic pointed to the fox which was then—a century ago—doing a good job of holding Britain's rabbits in check. Rounded up in Somerset and Devonshire, a shipment of foxes —somewhat shaken by their long voyage—seemed to be the answer to the ranchers' prayers.

But things didn't work out as planned. Australia's scattered farmhouses and settlements are set in the midst of vast sheep ranges. Imported foxes found mutton more to their liking than rabbit—so killed lambs instead of bunnies.

One after another, European foes of the rabbit were brought into the Australian struggle. Weasels and ferrets killed a few—but concentrated on poultry. So did the much-touted mongoose. Snakes were highly recommended; imported and released, they proved useless. Owls and buzzards failed to thrive in the new continent.

By 1887 it was apparent that no ordinary measures would turn the tide. So a governmental commission offered a reward of 25,000 pounds sterling for "any method or process not previously known in the colony for the effective extermination of the rabbit."

No one ever claimed the reward. Strychnine was poured into water holes—but did more harm to sheep than to rabbits. Gangs of workmen made mass attacks upon long-established burrows; the cost of digging to the bottom of eight-foot runways proved prohibitive. Poison gas was pumped into warrens to kill thousands—but survivors multiplied so fast that ranks were soon replenished.

Launched well before the turn of the century, programs of fence building seemed to promise control even though eradication was not possible. Queensland ranchers discovered that fences were hardly in place before furry foes began digging under shallow barriers and climbing over low ones. After 6303 miles of fencing was erected in the region, it was declared too flimsy to serve its purpose.

By now, pressure of the expanding rabbit population was sending a trickle of hungry explorers across the great desert into western Australia. In 1901, alarmed lawmakers of that region launched the biggest fence-building program ever undertaken. Determined to repel the hopping invaders, men erected a special barrier that was buried deep in the ground and projected forty inches above the surface.

In order to serve its purpose, the fence would have to isolate an entire section of the continent. So it was built from one coastal point to another, which lay 1139 miles away. By the time the barrier was finished in 1907, rabbits were thriving well west of it. So armed guards were assigned to 100-mile sectors and sent on daily patrol. In desert regions, fence riders made their rounds on camel back.

But it was only a rear-guard maneuver to hold the line against new waves when the four-legged foes had already filtered past. A second fence was built seventy-five miles inside the original ring of wire. It proved a useful remedy but less than an all-out cure. So a third line was erected inside the others as a last-ditch defense of the great wheat belt.

No one knows precisely how many thousands of miles of rabbit fence were erected.

Almost as typically Australian as Merino sheep, the barriers for a time seemed to offer hope of human victory in the long-drawn contest. But a single pair of animals, squeezing through a fence while tiny, could grow up to repopulate a region once cleared of the foe. In time, most fences were abandoned as useless.

Direct damage to Australian grazing lands mounted to a toll of some $60,000,000 each year in wool losses alone. Long-range damage could not be measured. During periods of drought, hungry rabbits cut bark from scrub trees and literally cleared the land of small vegetation. Denuded regions, washed by later rains, eroded to become new deserts. Meanwhile, the plague spread to New Zealand and New South Wales.

Biologists versed in history might have said, "We told you so." For whenever a state of natural balance has been disturbed by the introduction of a new species or elimination of established predators, trouble has followed. Few creatures have left so long and wide a trail of destruction as the European rabbit—closely related to the U.S. cottontail, and more distantly kin to the jack rabbit of western plains.

Established in Spain and North Africa many centuries ago, the fast-multiplying creature was a favorite delicacy on Roman tables. Conquerors took bunnies to the Balearic Islands in the second century. Released, their fast-mounting hordes of progeny stripped big regions of all vegetation and dug burrows so vast that buildings were undermined.

Before the New World was discovered, Prince Henry the Navigator reasoned that it would have to be colonized with domestic animals. So he experimented by establishing rabbits on Porto Santo. Two years after they were turned loose in 1419, their descendants ate the island bare and made it unfit for human colonization.

Since the famous Domesday Book mentions neither rabbits nor their warrens, many historians believe Normans introduced the animals to Britain. During the days of Robin Hood, forests sheltered so many flesh-eating birds and animals that rabbits remained scarce and costly.

Six pence—standard price for a suckling pig—was the value

of a fourteenth-century bunny. When Ralph de Borne was installed as abbot of Canterbury cathedral in 1309, the banquet table was loaded with 600 fat rabbits.

A standard figure in folk tales, a prized game animal for centuries, and a foe to be tolerated during many generations, the rabbit has recently launched a biological blitz in Britain. For the twentieth-century decrease in populations of owls and foxes, weasels and hawks has brought trouble. An estimated 100,000,000 rabbits slashed into field crops, ate the heart out of pastures by selective feeding, reduced the length of the grazing season, and attacked wild seedlings along with nursery stock.

Net result: economists agreed that of all animal problems, the cost of maintaining Britain's rabbits soared to a point just under that of her rat population.

Compensating factors reduced the toll—by a fraction.

Australia began exporting frozen rabbits in 1894. That year, 14,928 entered world trade. Two decades later, the annual flow into European markets was more than 10,000,000 animals. Rabbit meat has brought Australia more export dollars than either beef or mutton. Long the backbone of the felt-hat industry, rabbit hair was the chief ingredient in 32,000,000 "digger" hats worn by Aussies in World War II.

Domestic strains gave France a meat-and-fur industry of some importance; in England, 40,000,000 wild rabbits entered commerce each year. In dollar volume, rabbit skins were second only to wool in Australian trade with the United States. Dyed and trimmed to simulate expensive furs, Br'er Rabbit's coat is sold under more than one hundred different trade names. Because good luck comes to the possessor of the left hind foot of a graveyard cottontail caught in the dark of the moon, several U.S. firms process millions of rabbit feet each year.

All told, world returns from wild rabbit populations have never accounted for as much as one fifth the damage inflicted upon agriculture.

So man's counterattack has continued without armistice. In its most recent and most successful phase, the war on rabbits has been pursued along biological planes. By making use of an organism that reproduces even more rapidly than the rabbit, ranks of the nibbling foe have been greatly thinned.

Clues leading to the discovery of the organic weapon were first uncovered—not in Australia or England, but in South America. Laboratory rabbits of a Montevideo scientist became sick and died in 1898. Investigation revealed that they had contracted a malady common to the native South American rabbit, or tapeti. Tapeti nearly always recovered from myxomatosis—but the illness was nearly 100 per cent fatal to its distant cousin, the domestic rabbit.

Preserved in scientific records, these findings created no excitement until 1928. That year, a South American biologist had a brainstorm. Myxomatosis is lethal in the case of white rabbits of the laboratory, he reasoned. All strains of domestic rabbits are descended from the European wild rabbit.

Therefore . . . myxomatosis should prove the key to victory over the hordes in Australia.

Experiments were launched, not only there, but also in Britain and Scandinavia. All failed. Something was wrong—but no one knew what it might be. Though animals injected in the laboratory always died within a week or ten days, the disease did not spread through wild populations. This promising lead had developed into one more blind alley.

Though their work seemed futile, staff members of the Australian Commonwealth Scientific and Industrial Research Organization continued to inject the South American virus into rabbits, many of which were turned loose on sheep ranges. Six or seven 1950 trials produced the same old result: infected animals died, but the malady did not spread to their fellows.

Then came sudden action.

From one more experiment performed in routine fashion, myxomatosis became epidemic among rabbit hordes along a major water course. What could account for the difference? Probing, searching, and inquiring, scientists concluded that the key to the spread of the malady was abnormally high concentrations of mosquitoes in a flooded area.

Eventually it became clear that the rabbit-killing virus is transmitted in mechanical fashion. Laboratories rely on infected pins; under natural conditions, mouth parts of biting insects play the same role. Mosquitoes and sand flies performed nobly in Australia; reaching France and England, the malady was spread by rabbit fleas of types seldom found outside Europe.

During a three-year period, Australia's rabbit population was reduced by 96 per cent; wool production jumped more than $50,000,000 a year above earlier levels. In parts of England, myxomatosis leveled 99.5 per cent of the bunnies in woods and fields; crop yields rose as much as 50 per cent.

Introduced to France by Dr. Armand-Delille, the disease worked such havoc that hunters and furriers banded together to sue the scientist for damages. Meanwhile, the Pasteur Institute developed a serum by which domestic rabbits could be immunized.

Given a few decades, wild rabbits probably will not need it. For in spite of a smashing victory at the mid-point of the twentieth century, man has by no means exterminated his nibbling foe.

Even when myxomatosis was making its most dramatic advances, biologists brought up theoretical arguments against its long-continued success. Instability is likely to mark any relationship in which a parasite kills 99 per cent of its hosts, they reasoned. Given a few generations, changes in rabbit or virus could reduce the mortality rate—and resistant bunnies could multiply to regain their old status.

After all, rabbits have been around for quite a while. With opossums, they rank as the most ancient surviving mammals of North America. Fossil remains of types not greatly different from those of today have been found in rocks 60,000,000 years old. Man is a biological youngster who has been on the scene only a fraction of that time.

Viewed in terms of years or decades, man's victory seems decisive. But in terms of centuries and millennia, no one can predict what may come. By 1954, there was evidence of growing immunity among rabbits of Australia. The next year, strains of resistant animals seemed to be emerging in Nottinghamshire.

Given a little time—a mere thousand years or so—the bunny blitz could conceivably hit once more with many times its former fury.

Strange Revenge of the Flying Axman

Todd Pfitzenmeyer, graduate student at Pennsylvania State University, was recently asked to try to learn to think like a pileated woodpecker. If he succeeds, he may discover why the Paul Bunyan of birds is riddling utility poles.

Four major power companies have joined forces to sponsor research in the psychology of woodpeckers. Their grant to Penn State was made in the hope that specialists could discover some way to stem the rising tide of damage by feathered choppers.

Villain of the piece is the big *Ceophloeus pileatus,* whose name stems from the fact that his head is topped with a big cap or *pileus*. Some of his less flashy cousins were revered by the ancients. Still, nothing in woodpecker history rivals the current surge of interest growing out of the bird's campaign against artificial trees on which men string wires to transmit power and communications. Recent months have seen him subject of a cover story in *Electric World,* discussed in *Chemical Week,* and featured on page one of the *Wall Street*

Journal. Not bad for a redheaded fellow who is really a country boy at heart.

Woodpeckers are found throughout the world, except in Australia and Madagascar. But because Britain has only three species, early explorers were startled by the number and variety of types they found in the New World.

Many are brightly marked and noisy, but only two are conspicuously large. Now seldom seen, the ivorybill is among the most striking of land birds. Its cousin, the troublemaking pileated, is smaller and duller but similar in many details.

His chisel-shaped beak poised for a shattering blow on the target of the moment, a full-grown male may measure eighteen inches in length. Wingspread averages slightly more than two feet. Most plumage is dusty blackish, but white throat and stripes down the side of the neck give a rakish look to the red-capped fellow. His white wing linings, conspicuous in flight, make identification easy.

It is an unforgettable experience to see one of the feathered loggers at work. On still days, noise of his chopping can be heard a mile and a half. Just one precisely directed blow may knock out a chip as big as a pencil. Careful observers vow that in one working day a single bird can drive a nine-inch by five-inch hole into the heart of a two-foot tree.

Plains and grasslands are not suitable for these birds, for they feed chiefly on wood-boring insects. Larvae of beetles, harbored under bark and in tunnels gnawed into living trees, are favorite delicacies. So are other types of grubs found in stumps and rotting logs. Big black carpenter ants, which riddle the heartwood of many a beech and white pine, form a staple item of diet.

Early decades of the nineteenth century saw the beginning of a bizarre conflict. Swinging axes and pulling crosscut saws, settlers cleared land with reckless abandon. Cutting of the forests meant war—an all-out attack by humans who seemed bent upon eliminating essentials for woodpecker life. It was man against bird, and no quarter to the vanquished.

Changes were too rapid and extensive for the exotic ivory-bill. It was in full-scale retreat by 1850. Since then, numbers have continued to shrink until the giant woodpecker has become one of the rarest of North American birds.

According to logic, precisely the same fate should have come to its pileated cousin. Instead, science and industry are now seeking ways to overcome economic threats posed by the stubborn chopper.

Most varieties of woodpeckers are equipped with distinctive tools for clinging and cutting. Hence some features of the pileated are much like those of his cousins. Each of his toes bears a long, curved claw ending in a sharp tip. Two toes of each foot point forward, while the other two point backward. Thrust into wood or bark and drawn tight by muscles, this apparatus operates much like a set of old-fashioned ice hooks. Pressure serves to drive the hold tighter; even after death a bird may cling to the tree or pole he last attacked.

Six sets of paired feathers form the all-important tail of the crimson-topped woodsman. All except the outer pair are long and stiff, forming a spring-like lever. Thrust against the surface of his perch, the woodpecker's tail becomes a brace.

Members of the species have one of the strangest tools operated by any bird—a long, flexible tongue shaped like an angleworm. Its horny tip is flanked by two rows of tiny barbs. Capable of extending more than three inches past the end of the beak, the tongue serves as a harpoon.

Like man's most advanced models, the woodpecker's weapon is equipped with automatic recoil devices. Muscles serve to eject the tongue, while tiny bones yank it back when the target is hit. When foraging for ants rather than grubs, the bird is helped by a glue-like saliva that covers the entire tongue. An insect touched by the viscous stuff is trapped; struggle as he may, he seldom succeeds in pulling free.

Pileateds differ from their relatives in the make-up of beak and skull. Because several cubic inches of wood may intervene between a hungry bird and its waiting dinner, an efficient cutting tool is a necessity.

Shaped like a sturdy chisel, the beak is almost equally well adapted for chipping, gouging, and splitting. Like nails and teeth of humans, it is a special modification from cells of the skin. Hence, like skin, it grows throughout life. Damage from incessant pounding is counteracted by the natural processes of repair. Even when the entire tip of a bird's bill is broken off, it grows back quickly.

The peculiar structure of their skull bones may account for the fact that the birds do not become punch-drunk. Most feathered creatures have skulls made light by air pockets. In the case of pileated woodpeckers, this trait is accentuated so that the delicate brain case forms a shock-absorbing "poem in bone."

His special skull, beak, tongue, feet, and tail combine to make the colorful flier efficient at just one task: digging into wood for beetles and ants. To the degree that any species is equipped to function in a narrow environment, its capacity for survival is believed linked with preservation of the status quo. Change external conditions to which its ways are geared, and a bird or animal is likely to dwindle to extinction.

That is just what seems to have happened in the case of the ivory-billed woodpecker. Dependent upon conditions that prevail in vast tracts of big timber, ranks of the bird were thinned along with forests. Since the pileated woodpecker long made its home in precisely the same stands of great trees, experts concluded that its days were also numbered.

A rapid decline in the bird's numbers began shortly before the Civil War. By 1875, naturalists were registering concern over the possibility of its extinction. As trees were felled at increasingly rapid rates, it became a matter of considerable interest to find one pileated woodpecker in Pennsylvania, Illinois, or Michigan.

Slowly but steadily the big birds began a comeback. Perhaps the tide turned during the first decade of the new century, for in 1916 a Canadian outdoorsman joyfully reported having seen thirty-four of them in a five-year period. General increases over much of the continent were noted during the 1920s. Population probably doubled in the fifteen years that followed the end of the flapper era, then doubled again between 1945 and 1955.

Changed habits are believed responsible for the strange upward surge.

Once found only in thick forests of big timber, the pileated now nests in many thin woods and groves of small second-growth trees. Long prone to flee from areas invaded by settlers, the bird has become a familiar sight in villages and small towns of the Southeast. One pair was found nesting within five miles of the Empire State Building.

Though vigilant in searching for grubs and ants, today's crested woodpecker probably eats less insects and more vegetable matter than did those of pre-Columbian days. Seeds of the hackberry, wild grape, sumac, poison ivy, and Virginia creeper are of some importance in its diet. Carpenter ants are less plentiful than formerly—but part of the loss is made up by resorting to plowed fields where corn borers are to be had for the taking. In Georgia, pileated fellows have even started eating pecans.

All these factors point to the probability that the winged woodcutter has altered his ways in such fashion that he can more than hold his own. Though unchanged in anatomy, he is on the increase in a man-shaped environment quite different from the range of his ancestors.

Perhaps the pileated woodpecker's attack upon utility poles is a side effect linked with other changes in habit. Pole damage by the bird was first noted in 1906, more as a curiosity than a matter of concern. As population increased, the vandalism curve moved sharply upward. By 1950 it was a subject of conversation at nearly every meeting of executives in the pole industry.

In many respects, the experience of the Pennsylvania Power and Light Company is typical. Though a nuisance, woodpecker damage to the system was confined to small areas as late as 1943–46. Yearly costs of replacing bird-weakened poles tripled between 1946 and 1953. No longer confined to a few local sections, it spread over miles of lines and mounted to a toll of $15,000 a year.

Feathered cutters are costing New Jersey Power and Light more than $5000 a year. Connecticut Power and Light is beginning to have serious problems. Damage has been reported from areas as far apart as Alabama and Oregon. Normally good for thirty-five years, the life expectancy of poles in trouble spots has dropped as low as two years. In some swamps, the replacement of a single pole may cost a thousand dollars.

In theory, the use of hardware cloth seemed an obvious solution. Poles can be wrapped with it at small cost; it should stop anything softer than a cold chisel. It actually did discourage Mississippi woodpeckers. For some reason, they tend to run well below average in size. Big birds of Pennsylvania took the barrier in stride, soon showed they could rip half inch nineteen-gauge steel mesh from any pole shielded with it.

Plastic and rubberized coatings fared no better. So linemen have tried more than fifty different chemicals that offered hope as repellents. One of them sent rabbits scurrying off in haste, but none had a significant effect upon woodpeckers. Desperate, pole users in Louisiana turned to expensive imported woods. Even South American greenheart, more than three times as hard as domestic timbers, was quickly riddled.

Imitation snakes were fashioned from green hose, then draped about poles. After the first cautious visit to a section of line decorated in this fashion, birds paid no attention to reptiles. Red-flannel streamers were nailed to test poles. Pileated attackers ripped the cloth to shreds, used some of it to line their nests. Shiny whirlers such as the kind favored by used-car dealers actually did frighten the vandals—for a few days. Stuffed owls mounted along a test section didn't last as long as the metal whirlers.

A new dimension was added to the puzzle when study showed that the pileated seldom cuts a hole in sound portions of a live tree. In the forest, the bird concentrates on injured areas of live trees and insect-infested portions of dead ones. The value of his services as an exterminator far overshadows the cost of his vandalism.

There's always the chance that he whacks poles for the fun of it. Regardless of motive, his campaign is bringing strange retribution upon the two-legged creature who so recently cut the woodpeckers' trees.

That Filthy Beast, the Ape

Diverse as they are in structure and habits, bears and guinea pigs, rabbits and mules are alike in one respect: each species gains its importance from its role as a competitor or ally of its fellow creature, *Homo sapiens*. All trails blazed through the wonderful and mysterious regions of natural history converge upon the organism whose members not only struggle for existence, but also search for understanding.

Lecturing before the Philosophical Institute of Edinburgh, Thomas Huxley reduced the quest for knowledge to a single issue. "The question of questions for mankind," he said, "—the problem which underlies all others, and is more deeply interesting than any other—is the ascertainment of the place which Man occupies in nature and of his relations to the universe of things. Whence our race has come; what are the limits of our power over nature, and of nature's power over us; to what goal we are tending; are the problems which present themselves anew and with undiminished interest to every man born into the world."

Modern striving for answers to that "question of questions"

has been largely guided by attempts to uncover the riddles of the great apes.

Neither the gorilla nor the chimpanzee nor the orangutan has ever been a serious competitor of man; except in the modern manufacture of pharmaceuticals, these creatures have made no significant contribution to human welfare. Yet they symbolize inquiry into the origin and meaning of our own species. Hence no other animals have evoked a corresponding storm of controversy in laboratories and cathedrals, museums and courts of justice.

All the man-like apes are confined to limited regions far from centers of civilization. So until this century, scholars and scientists had few opportunities to study them.

History's first mention of anthropoids dates from 470 B.C. That year, Hanno the Carthaginian set out with a great fleet of fifty-oared galleys in an attempt to colonize northern Guinea. Scouts who explored regions about the coast came into contact with queer hairy creatures who ran upright and jabbered in a harsh dialect. Nobody could be positive whether these strangers were animals who resembled men or primitive tribesmen with traits of beasts.

Several of the odd little "women" were killed; skins of two were taken to the temple of Astarte and exhibited there until the Roman invasion of 146 B.C. It is all but certain that they were chimpanzees.

Occasional specimens were brought to European and African cities. Intrigued and horrified, the great Cicero summed up the reaction of many first encounters: "How like to us is that filthy beast the ape." Until the mid-point of the nineteenth century, the animals that seem caricatures of men were regarded as curiosities but had no important place in thought.

Religious leaders and scientists recognized that there are

many riddles about the origin of man and his fellow creatures, of course. But speculative philosophy rather than laboratory investigation was the path followed in seeking answers.

Questions abounded: Why are there so many different kinds of living things? How did the species come into existence? What is man's relationship to other organisms whose bodies have more or less in common with his own? How long have animals and men lived on our planet? What is the process by which the mating of a male and female produces new life cast into the same form as that of its parents?

Orthodox thinkers—in science as well as in religion—were content with an all-inclusive answer: all the kinds of life were formed in a single act by divine creation; each species has its fixed pattern that is changeless throughout all time.

Inevitably, some Christian scholars used the Scriptures as a textbook of history and biology as well as religion. Dr. John Lightfoot, vice-chancellor of Cambridge University, issued a momentous report in 1654. Having made a scrupulous study of all dates recorded in Holy Writ, he had solved the riddle of the date at which the earth and its inhabitants were formed. "Heaven and earth, centre and circumference were made in the same instance of time, and clouds full of water and man were created by the Trinity on the 26th of October, 4004 B.C., at 9:00 in the morning."

That should have settled the matter. . . .

For multitudes it did. But puzzling and even disturbing bits of evidence were beginning to accumulate. Medieval focus upon alchemy had given way to interest in living things; just before 1800, J. B. Lamarck proposed that all the phenomena of life be grouped into a bundle and made the subject matter of a new science to be called "biology."

Biologists soon discovered that animals and plants can be

divided into groups that are more or less distinct. Living forms are organized in a number of different ways—rather than built upon a single pattern that runs through all nature. Some creatures have external shells, while others have an internal framework of bones. Body temperature of reptiles varies widely with surroundings, but horses have a built-in regulator that keeps them at a constant level in summer and winter. Ducks hatch from eggs that show no sign of life, while kittens emerge from the body of their mother.

Moreover, careful observation of domestic animals over a period of a few generations showed that distinct changes occur; dogs bred for bullbaiting have faces quite unlike those of their ancestors. Could it be that the stream of life is fluid rather than frozen—involving establishment of new types rather than mechanical duplication of patterns fixed "in the beginning"?

Count Georges de Buffon thought so. The thick kneepads of camels, he argued, must have come about as a result of their constant kneeling. Generations of chafing against sand and rocks must have caused snakes to grow their protective scales.

Lamarck staked his reputation on a somewhat different theory. Organic change comes about as a fruit of desire and effort on the part of creatures, he suggested. Sustained yearning to swim produced the webbed feet of ducks, while the long necks of giraffes stem from attempts to reach leaves of tall trees! This view has the special merit of explaining such bodily features as the vermiform appendix of man—for is it not logical that if an organ enlarges through use, it will shrink from inactivity?

Though such theories soon proved to be false, growing numbers of naturalists came to recognize that organic change is a reality. Borrowing a technical term from early students of embryology, they used "evolution" as a label to name the "unwinding" process of nature that they did not fully understand. Most early evolutionists concurred in the erroneous belief that bodily changes made during the life of a creature may be transmitted to its offspring. Just what factor or force serves as the mainspring of the vast natural movement, few so much as wondered.

Young Charles Darwin was an exception. After being educated for the ministry at Edinburgh and Cambridge, he accepted an invitation to serve as naturalist on the surveying vessel, *Beagle*. Plants and animals of South America and Australasia fired his mind; he was especially intrigued by the giant turtles and strange fossils of the Galapagos Islands. How did these creatures come into existence? What forces determine which forms of life will survive and multiply at the expense of their competitors?

Darwin concentrated his entire energy upon the riddle of life. He collected specimens, experimented with inbreeding of animals, read every book that had bearing on the question.

One thin volume fell into his hands by chance. Published in 1798 by a country parson, it was almost wholly speculative. After all, what more could be expected of a youngster of twenty-two who lacked scientific training and had only the curiosity of an eager amateur?

Theoretical or not, the musings of Thomas Malthus were strangely provocative. For according to his *Essay on the Principle of Population*, man is engaged in a ceaseless "struggle for existence." Whenever population pressures reach a level too high for the food supply, numbers are reduced by famine, war, disease, or some other natural calamity.

This was it—the key! Organic competition for life's necessities, concluded Darwin, is as universal among plants and animals as among men. Survival of the fittest could be the clue to evolutionary change. . . .

Abundant evidence in his notes and letters indicates that this concept was matured in his thinking by the time the naturalist was thirty-five, in 1844. But instead of following the example of Malthus and rushing to produce a volume of speculations, Darwin decided to accumulate data. Someday he would write a thick book that no man could challenge; it would establish the truth that species change and evolve through natural selection.

Nothing so radical here, it seems. But wait . . . Man himself is a biological organism. He belongs within the same stream of life that holds all other creatures. Does this new theory affect views about the theory-forming animal?

From the beginning of his inquiry, Charles Darwin knew that his ideas were revolutionary. He recognized that the accepted view of creation would be challenged, that estimates of man's place and significance in nature would be scrutinized in minute detail. Perhaps it was his reluctance to start an intellectual war that deterred him from publicizing his views; perhaps it was eagerness to be wholly accurate. He was jolted into sudden action by one of the most bizarre sets of events in the history of modern thought.

Early in 1857—thirteen years after developing his concept of evolution—Darwin began corresponding with a naturalist nearly twenty years his junior. Alfred Russell Wallace, busy collecting plant and animal specimens in the Malay Archipelago, had been inspired by Darwin's early *Journal of Researches.* So he began sending letters and specimens, asking questions, airing his own views. Almost from the beginning of their acquaintance, both men recognized that they were attacking the same problem from similar points of view.

June 18, 1858, brought Darwin a thick letter posted from the island of Ternate. It included a brief essay, which Wallace hoped his friend would transmit to editors for publication. Entitled "The Tendency of Varieties to Depart Infinitely from the Original Type," it left Darwin "quite prostrated"—for his friend's paper dealt with the principle he had pondered during nearly two decades.

Duly transmitted and published without arousing much stir, the Wallace paper stimulated Darwin to present his own material to the public. Hastily abstracting from the mass of his long-planned "big book," he prepared a discussion *On the Origin of Species by Means of Natural Selection.*

Scheduled to appear in November 1859, the little volume was not expected to evoke great interest. Publishers proposed an edition of 1250 copies; Darwin considered this too ambitious. But when it went on sale, the entire edition was exhausted the first day.

Apes are not mentioned in the carefully phrased little book, nor is there any suggestion that apes and men are near relatives. Darwin deliberately avoided emphases that could lead to theological argument; he intended to say nothing at all about man. But feeling that silence would seem cowardly or dishonest, he reluctantly inserted a suggestion that his ideas would throw light on the origin and history of mankind.

Victorians reacted far more violently than did readers to whom the Kinsey reports were presented. Like the latter, the *Origin of Species* is a semi-technical work not intended for the general public. It contains nothing that faintly resembles purple passages of sensational novels. There is no direct statement concerning man's place in nature or the manner of man's development. Apes are not treated. Yet the treatise was immediately dubbed "The Monkey Book."

Thomas Huxley defended his friend's views in a famous debate with Samuel Wilberforce, bishop of Oxford. Queried as to whether he counted himself descended from an ape on his grandfather's side or his grandmother's, the scientist retorted that a monkey in his family tree would do him more honor than a bishop.

Punch devoted whole columns to evolution. Scientific terms became household slogans. Folk who had no understanding of technical issues snatched copies of the *Origin* from bookshops as though it were lurid fiction. Dramatists incorporated biological data in popular plays; Charles Kingsley even punctuated *Water-Babies* with evolutionary arguments.

Mrs. Darwin never became reconciled to her husband's views. Sir Charles Lyell, most distinguished geologist of the day, admitted that he shuddered at the notion of man's descent from apes. Asa Gray, internationally renowned botanist, gave intellectual assent to Darwin's conclusions—but grimaced at recognizing that "the very first step backward makes the Negro and the Hottentot our blood relations."

No scientific debate in history, not even that which followed the publication of Copernicus' *De Revolutionibus*, has evoked an emotional storm like that which broke over the heads of "the ape man" and his followers. Intensity of the conflict stemmed from several streams of intellectual change that converged on the central question of man's origin and meaning.

Modern literary interpretation of the Bible was launched in 1780. Just one generation before Darwin's birth, German theologian Johann Eichhorn issued a revolutionary analysis of Old Testament historical books. For the first time it was suggested to the Hebrew-Christian world that Moses did not write the entire text of the books that bear his name. By 1833, evidence was discovered which indicated several "editors" played a part in the preparation of the ancient documents.

Debated with vigor over a period of several decades, this issue was at the boiling point when the *Origin* appeared. Hence many prominent men—including William Gladstone—

attacked the theory of evolution because it seemed to challenge views of Scripture that were being defended against "German scholarship."

Closely related to purely literary studies that shook long-established ideas about Holy Writ, there came a series of historical finds. Modern archaeology of biblical lands began in 1798, when Napoleon Bonaparte brought a company of artists and scholars to the valley of the Nile. Hieroglyphic inscriptions were first deciphered in 1822, and the cuneiform script of the ancients became intelligible in 1846.

That was just two years after Count Konstantin von Tischendorf found a very early manuscript of Old Testament portions. Discovered in a Mount Sinai monastery, it became a treasure of the Russian government and attracted world interest. Ancient handwritten sheets of this *Codex Sinaiticus* led to no major revisions of words and phrases in Scripture. Archaeological finds eventually supported the historical accuracy of the Bible, rather than refuting it. Still, popular thought was in a ferment comparable to that brought about by the later finding of the Dead Sea Scrolls.

More fuel was added to the fire by queer bone fragments uncovered in the cave of Neanderthal—a ravine of the Neander River near Düsseldorf. Germans who studied them were convinced that the pieces were human in origin; yet huge ridges across the cranium seemed to hint of some strange sub-human whose head was shaped like that of man. Amateurs insisted that the skull was that of a Russian soldier killed during the Napoleonic Wars; many specialists held that it was quite ordinary except for modifications brought about by disease.

Though he lacked anything approaching formal proof, Thomas Huxley spoke up. These bones, he declared, came from a primitive man who lived long before the dawn of civilization—tens of centuries before the date some religionists accepted as the time of earth's creation.

From the day he first read the *Origin*, young Huxley had expected a fight. He warned Darwin that abuse and misrepresentation would be heaped upon him, suggested that the combativeness of his friends might stand him in good stead. "I am sharpening up my claws and beak in readiness," he promised.

Far more pugnacious than Darwin, his friend was himself a scientist of note. At nineteen he discovered at the base of human hairs a membrane that textbooks still label "Huxley's layer." At twenty his examination for the medical degree was passed with such distinction that a gold medal was awarded. Six years later he was made a Fellow of the Royal Society.

It was this brilliant and ambitious young celebrity who enjoyed calling himself "Darwin's bulldog." More than any other man connected with the scientific revolution, he went out of his way to attack the complacent in science as well as in religion.

Darwin had deliberately side-stepped the issue of man's evolution. Very well, his bulldog would bare his teeth at the enemy. In 1863, Huxley published a volume on *Man's Place in Nature*, in which he declared that *Homo sapiens* is as fully within the evolutionary stream as the lowest mollusk.

Correctly as it happened, though without adequate evidence, he argued that the Neanderthall skull pointed to a very ancient human type with ape-like anatomical features. It was not until 1886 when two more such skulls were found in a Belgian cave that Huxley's brilliant guess was shown to be accurate.

Meanwhile, public interest in the relation of beasts to men was greatly stimulated by still another influence: a fast-swelling flow of data about mysterious man-like creatures of the Dark Continent.

Early in the seventeenth century, an obscure English adventurer spent some years in the Congo, came home with stories about "a kinde of Great Apes, of the height of a man, but twice as bigge in feature of their limmes, with strength proportionable, hairie all over, otherwise altogether like men and women in their whole bodily shape." Comparatively few persons read that description, and no one seems to have taken it seriously.

So it was just twelve years before publication of the *Origin* that a startled England had its first proof that apes bigger than the chimpanzee are real rather than mythical creatures.

Limited to a restricted region of interior Africa, the gorilla never has been numerous. Even native hunters seldom kill a specimen; small wonder that no white man gained such a prize until the forbidden continent was opened by missionaries. Dr. Thomas Savage, missionary on the Gabon, sent drawings and a skull to the anatomist Owen in 1847. Four years later, a nearly complete skeleton reached Philadelphia; several fragments were sent to Paris in the meantime.

Popular interest ran high. Newspapers and magazines published detailed accounts of every find; amateurs leaped to the conclusion that today's gorillas represent a retarded branch of the human family. Sir William Flower proved to his own satisfaction and that of a distinguished Cambridge audience the "existence in apes of those cerebral characters which have been said to be peculiar to man."

Huxley made the most of the furor.

When the first embalmed gorilla reached England in 1859, he was triumphant. Though he had a limited understanding of their anatomy and no firsthand knowledge of their habits, he wrote an essay "On the Natural History of the Man-like

Apes." First of three sections in his study of man's place in nature, it gave him a base from which to argue that "man is, in substance and in structure, one with the brutes." Lower forms of apes, he insisted, are further removed from the great apes than are the latter from men.

Structural resemblances actually are astonishing; orang and chimpanzee, gorilla and man seem to be cut from about the same biological pattern. None of these creatures has a tail; all of them can walk erect. We have the same number of fingers, toes, and teeth. Among all four species, gestation is a nine-month period. All the primates are equipped with an appendix, and members of each group sometimes snore!

Both men and apes have opposable thumbs and flattened nails on fingers and toes. Structure of the collarbone is remarkably similar among all primates. Large brains and an elaborate vocal mechanism characterize the entire group. Human traits of apes are so pronounced that native names stress them; *orangutan,* for example, is a dialect term meaning "man of the woods."

Absorbed in a soul-possessing quest for new truth and limited in data about both the great apes and fossil men, it is small wonder that Huxley and his fellows stressed resemblances and minimized differences between the species they studied. Nearly all their conclusions rested on anatomical details. They gave little attention to intellectual and cultural factors, compared specific bones and organs but failed to analyze total biosocial organisms.

Subsequent analysis has revealed major differences that were overlooked or minimized in the early excitement over gross resemblances between men and apes.

No other primate has a spinal column with the S-like curvature characteristic of man's. Gorilla, chimpanzee, and orang differ from us by their lack of a chin. One of man's most pronounced structures—a rounded and elevated forehead—is not remotely approached by any species of ape. All apes are heavily clothed in hair; man's is largely concentrated on his head. Human feet have the same bones as those of an ape, but the two are constructed on quite different architectural principles. The number of teeth is constant through most of the primate series, but the arrangement in man's mouth is radically and characteristically unique.

Early in the analysis of skeletons, anatomists concluded that man's upright posture is reflected in his entire frame. Even a small fragment of bone has clues that tell the specialist whether it came from a man or an ape. Hence the total organism, man, differs greatly from the total organism, gorilla.

Some of the differences do not appear from the study of bones alone. A famous drawing by Huxley compares skeletons of orang and chimpanzee, gorilla and man. Individual bones in his sketch are approximately accurate in both form and proportions. But "Darwin's bulldog" drew man in a slightly stooped position and apes in abnormally erect postures!

He is not to be censured for minimizing differences in this fashion, for he had no opportunity to study apes in their native habitats.

Forced by circumstances to rest his case largely upon bones —the only evidence available—it is small wonder that he failed to give due weight to non-physical factors. Huxley and his contemporaries knew, of course, that man's brain is more than twice as large as that of any living ape. They recognized, but did not stress, man's unique capacity to communicate by means of words and other abstract symbols. They were unaware that apes cannot be domesticated or that animals which are docile and alert in their early years seem to suffer "arrested development" and never progress past a low moronic stage.

Knowledge of the great apes is now many times as extensive as in the heyday of excitement over their relationship with men. It is significant that they make a very poor showing when faced with the supreme biological test: survival and multiplication. Structurally very close to man, the gorilla is found only in tropical Africa and has long been threatened with extinction. Though more numerous and spread over a larger portion of equatorial Africa, the chimpanzee is numerically insignificant. The orang is found only on the islands of Borneo and Sumatra.

Fossil records suggest that no species of great ape has ever been numerous. There is no indication that any member of the family has given man significant trouble—to say nothing of serious challenge—in the struggle for mastery of the planet. And in spite of his varied structural and mental resources, the ape has proved useless to man except as a subject of inquiry and a specimen for exhibition to the curious.

Archaeology has made great strides in the century since Darwin set the world agog. Mounting numbers of finds in Africa and Asia, as well as in Europe, have clarified the evolutionary paths of both men and apes. Today, no serious scientist supports the notion that humans are descendants of living anthropoid species—to say nothing of the long-popular view that negroes sprang from gorillas, mongolians from orangs, and whites from chimpanzees!

New fossil finds plus more accurate dating by means of radio carbon and other recent techniques have given conclusive proof that man is far older than any Victorian dared guess. Peking man, one of several human species long extinct, seems to have been using bone tools and fire some 400,000 to 600,000 years ago. Even Neanderthal man, whose skullcap was ammunition for Huxley's assault upon the taken-for-granted, is no longer considered to have been a direct ancestor of *Homo sapiens*.

Most specialists now think that modern man, several extinct human groups, and today's great apes are descendants from an unknown type of primate that thrived at least 30,000,000 years ago. Vague and scattered clues suggest that the family tree branched some 25,000,000 years ago. One line is thought to have produced the gibbon, while the other is believed to have continued toward human and ape types.

At least half a million years ago—and probably much earlier—still obscure genetic changes led to the appearance of *Homo erectus*. Much like humans of today in anatomy, this shadowy figure of the past walked erect, but his skull capacity was little greater than that of some apes. Since only bony structures have been preserved, it is futile to speculate concerning the degree to which his brain showed the unique convolutions that are a trademark of modern man.

Long extinct, this early human was followed by big-brained *Homo sapiens*, to which species belong all the varied races of men. Size of the human brain case seems to have changed but little in 100,000 years—but there have been radical transformations in shape, leading to today's characteristic high, rounded forehead and oval skull.

"Evolution" is no longer a fighting word. Significant only in the realm of ideas, the great apes have seen their day. After having been brought to the Western world just a century ago and dividing Christendom into hostile camps, they have been permitted to pad back to jungle and zoo. Understanding of their place in natural history once threatened to debase man and remove him from his central significance among organisms. Maturing knowledge has led to a new understanding of the grandeur of the creature who is unique as asker of questions and finder of answers about animals and men.

Nature's Living Surgical Knife

Soviet doctors prolonged their examinations as long as they dared, then gathered for consultation. One head after another nodded. No doubt about it; Joseph Stalin had suffered hemorrhage of the brain. With the eyes of the world focused on his hospital bed, the dying dictator was initiated into a society that includes half the titled figures of Western history.

In a desperate attempt to lower his blood pressure, leeches were twice applied to Stalin's body. In thus yielding his vital fluid to hungry sucking creatures, the Russian joined a company that includes Julius Caesar, Napoleon Bonaparte, Lord Nelson, Gustavus Adolphus, and the Duke of Wellington. Along with millions of patients whose names are now forgotten, these conquerors shed blood through incisions made by nature's living surgical knife.

A cold-blooded member of the worm tribe who has a yen for warm blood, the medicinal leech is in a class all by itself. Nearly all man's use of his fellow creatures has centered upon directing their labor or stuffing their carcasses down his gullet. Deliberate use of the human body as a cafeteria for competing species is not an everyday, run-of-the-mill activity.

As a standard practice of leading surgeons, leeching flourished for more than twenty centuries. Nearly all ancient and primitive cultures employed it. Yet the heyday of the lancet-jawed animal came in a time of enlightenment and at centers of scientific progress. Hospital records indicate that in the period just before the U. S. Civil War, leeches drank 200,000 pounds of human blood each year in Paris alone.

Like every other piece of physician's gear, the leech is strictly functional in significance. That is, use of the unique tool is linked with special theories of illness.

Recently developed concepts such as "stress" and "allergy" indicate how far we are from a full understanding of the ways our bodies can get out of order. Pasteur's revolutionary germ theory of disease, announced only a few decades ago, rests upon ideas quite foreign to classical medicine. Before men learned to fear the work of invading bacteria, many groups of maladies were regarded as due to evil spirits or to abnormal fluids released by body tissues.

What remedy, therefore, could be more logical than removing the source of the trouble? Whether a demon or a foul humor, it had to be taken from the body. That meant piercing the skin and drawing off the pain-making spirit or substance along with blood from the region involved.

Pliny, greatest of ancient naturalists, considered bloodletting too marvelous and profound an operation to be a human invention. It was revealed to men by the gods, he concluded, through agency of the hippopotamus.

Here is the terse account, as found in Book 8 of his famous *Natural History:* "When the animal has become too bulky by continued over-feeding, it goes down to the banks of the river and examines the reeds which have been newly cut; as soon as it has found a stump that is very sharp, it presses its body against it, and so wounds one of the veins in the thigh; and, by the flow of blood thus produced, the body, which would otherwise have fallen into a morbid state, is relieved."

Widely separated medical centers, some of which lacked the hippopotamus tradition, supported the conclusion that bloodletting can restore a morbid body to health.

Hemorrhage is now known to give temporary relief from some symptoms associated with fever diseases. It is anybody's guess as to the psychological effects of bleeding when both surgeon and patient considered it a sovereign remedy. In cultures as divergent as those of the Aztecs and the ancient Chinese, men and women cheerfully shed their blood for centuries in order to master pain and illness.

Even when a major pain spirit was released, though, direct opening of a vein was risky business. Before the beginning of written surgical manuals, direct techniques for cutting into blood vessels came into disrepute. Instead, physicians learned to make shallow wounds and withdraw blood through the skin by "cupping."

Successful cupping, with a minimum of scratches in the patient's epidermis, required some method for forcing the flow of blood. Greeks of the fourth century B.C. used a gourd. Held firmly over the site of treatment, air was exhausted through the neck of the instrument by suction.

American Indians arrived at an independent version of the same tool: a three-inch tip from a buffalo horn, with a hole for the medicine man's lips. Ancient Chinese never quite grasped the idea of the exhaust cup. So leading surgeons of the era used fine needles of steel, silver, or gold to make deep punctures which were squeezed to encourage the departure of pathological influences.

For a period before and after 300 B.C., teachers in the great medical school of Alexandria advised against universal bloodletting. Their voices were lost in the chorus of protests. Even the great Galen was a hearty advocate of cupping. He preferred glass instruments to the more common brass models, however, because he felt it wise to watch the actual flow.

Regardless of its composition, exhaustion of air from a cup was a vexatious problem. Suction by mouth was not fully satisfactory. Neither was it an amateur's task to burn tow inside a cup to heat the air before clapping it upon a patient's skin in such fashion that he wouldn't be scorched. Dozens of exhausting syringes were invented; none was entirely effective.

Nor could mechanical ingenuity quite cope with the problem of making the right kind of wound for widely varied sites of cupping. Early scarificators were crude affairs with one blade. More refined models included ten to sixteen lancets held by a setscrew so that the depth of the incisions could be regulated. Even in the case of elaborate models, a busy surgeon found it impossible to keep the blades free of rust.

So it was altogether natural that fainthearted ladies and noted physicians put a high premium upon the only bloodletting device whose fast and painless work left no messy instruments to wash.

Nicander of Colophon, a priest of Apollo in the second century B.C., made the earliest known clinical notes praising the leech as a surgeon's helper. He probably learned of the strange creature from traders who had visited India or Arabia. By the time of Augustus Caesar, most well-read European medical men were familiar with the animal. Pliny gave it the title *sanguisuga,* or bloodsucker.

Just how the creature received its modern name, no one knows. Most theories point to old Irish terms for a physician or conjurer as the root word. Saxons probably modified it into the form *leech* and used it as a title for any healer. Perhaps through two-way influence between terms for the healing worm and a practitioner of healing, the names emerged into modern speech in identical form. So the well-informed leech of medieval Europe was severely handicapped if he happened to be caught without a supply of leeches.

During many centuries, treatment by leeching was reserved for the wealthy who could afford to pay for so dainty a method of being bled. At no time did the Mediterranean region afford an adequate supply of the animals. For the most part, common folk had to be content with the barber-surgeon's knife, basin, and cup.

Yet there were ailments in which no other instruments could be substituted for leeches. For physicians came to attach increasing significance to the site of bloodletting, and it was awkward or impossible to apply cups to some body surfaces. Rhazes, foremost physician of Arabia in the tenth century, insisted that an abscess of the ear or inflammation of the nose had to be left untreated if leeches could not be had. Ninety years later that verdict was underscored and widely publicized in the medical encyclopedia compiled by Albucasis of Cordova.

In spite of the uncertain supply, demand for leeches mounted as they proved effective in increasing numbers of maladies. In conditions ranging from scabies to vertigo, from pleurisy to "Raving Madness," the bloodsucker proved its potency. Leaping 400 years ahead of public craving for obesity cures, Denis Heracleot won a kind of immortality in 1567. A woodcut of that date, included in *Histoires Prodigeuses,* portrays the fat fellow's benign smile as he sits with leech-covered arms and hands enjoying a treatment guaranteed to take pounds off his paunch.

Name your malady, and any competent physician could tell you how many leeches were needed and where they should be applied. For indigestion, twenty to thirty were placed at the pit of the stomach. Half a dozen on each temple constituted a sure cure for a cold. Infants having trouble with teething were treated by leeching behind the ears. Whooping cough required a substantial number applied to the abdomen. If extremely mild, an onset of gout might be countered by as few as four leeches on each ankle and one behind each ear—but high fever required a close-set band entirely around the head.

Two sets of influences converged late in the eighteenth century with the result that, almost overnight, the leech was catapulted from sedate dignity into a position of international prominence. One factor was fresh interpretation of medical theory, resulting in a new frenzy for bloodletting. A second influence was changed patterns of communication and transportation, fostering international trade in leeches.

Napoleon's rise to power made his nation the center of clinical medicine in Europe. Long reared commercially in the swamp regions of Bordeaux, leeches were abundant in France but during war became so scarce in England that they commanded prices as high as six shillings. No man alive had a higher opinion of the bloodsucking worm than did Francois Joseph Victor Broussais.

Three years an army surgeon under Napoleon, in 1831 Broussais became professor of general pathology at the Paris medical school. He considered gastroenteritis the basis of all illness—and the only effective remedy he knew was the application of leeches to stomach and head. Sometimes dubbed "the bloodiest physician in history," he used hundreds of leeches daily in his own practice—and taught his students to do the same.

French leechgrowers found themselves unable to keep up with the demand. Spain and Portugal were emptied, then Italy and Bohemia. Peasants learned to wade through bogs and marshes in order to emerge with a harvest of leeches clinging to their bare legs.

Importers sent agents into Poland, Russia, Bessarabia, Syria, and Turkey. Strasbourg became a regional collecting center; at the peak of the season, 60,000 to 80,000 leeches were forwarded to Paris each day. Importation into France reached a peak of about 57,500,000 animals each year. Still leading men of the nation's medical circles wrote articles urging farmers to divert their marshlands to leech culture. Prices had jumped from 12–15 francs in 1806 to 150–280 francs just half a century later, they noted.

Britain caught the fever in a form only slightly milder than that of France. In 1823, Europe exported 1,500,000 leeches to England and America. Next year, 5,000,000 went to England alone. Within a decade, the cost of leeches accounted for 5 per cent of the total annual expenditures of typical English hospitals. By 1842, a Norwich dealer considered himself understocked when he had less than 50,000 leeches on hand. Hospital use in London alone required 7,000,000 in 1863.

The frenzied catching of the animals thinned their numbers in Britain, then made them extinct. Russia saw a similar threat confronting her, so an 1848 edict established game laws for the leech. Collection was forbidden from May through July, and specimens less than two and five eighth inches long could not be shipped out of the country. Leech ponds sprang up everywhere—even in Moscow and St. Petersburg.

U.S. demand never passed the moderate level. Combined use of a native variety and fine ones imported from Europe accounted for 1,500,000 leeches each year for the half century that followed 1840. Wholesale prices seldom exceeded $100 per thousand. Most of the native supply came from the

Philadelphia region—especially the mud flats of the Delaware River.

Specialized study of the animal and its functions tended to focus in Europe. During the period 1700–1900, hundreds of technical papers were published. An elaborate mechanical leech was invented by M. Demours, but the monster never proved popular. Public interest in the living lancet reached such a peak that cloth manufacturers copied its color patterns, and many an expensive gown was decorated with replicas of the leech.

Excitement was limited to human ranks. Having no heart, the surgical animal experienced neither the pounding of excitement nor coronaries from ambitious striving. Since each individual is both a male and a female, fame brought no sexual maladjustments. At the height of their importance for men, leeches simply did the things for which their natural equipment prepares them superbly. They feasted on human blood and reared increasing numbers of little leeches.

Hirudo medicinalis, the medicinal leech of Europe and most important of the half dozen types used by physicians, looks much like a large varicolored earthworm. Soft browns, greens, and blacks blended in concealing patterns make the typical specimen all but invisible in its native environment. Waving gently in moving water, it seems to be a part of the background of water-soaked leaves and broken shadows.

Entirely lacking in appendages, the animal's body is divided into thirty-four segments, or rings. Six of them form a unit that includes the head and "mouth" of the creature, while a second body opening is included in the seven segments that form its caboose. Leeches swim gracefully, but on land can move only in inchworm fashion by using their suckers as gripping points.

Two to four inches long at maturity, the elastic leech can

stretch to ten inches or draw itself into a ball little bigger than an olive. Ten rudimentary eyes make it sensitive to lights and shadows, while other sense organs convey chemical and heat signals that help guide a prowling leech toward its prey.

In lieu of a heart, the animal has four pulsating veins. Oxygen is absorbed through the skin, for it has neither lungs nor gills.

Measured by conventional biological yardsticks, this creature is low in the scale of life—extremely simple by comparison with the red-blooded mammals on whom it prefers to feed in adult stages. Unlike its cousin, the earthworm, the leech has a very small body cavity and almost seems to be made up of two tubes, one inside the other.

Young leeches feed on eggs and larvae of other water creatures. Little-understood cycles of change upset this dietary pattern as the breeding season approaches. Though equipped with a muscle for opening and closing, the tiny throat becomes too narrow to admit solid food. So the mature leech goes hunting for blood.

Rear sucker fastened to a weed or stone, the hungry animal undulates in the water. Detecting clues that can lead it to prey, it relaxes its hold and swims toward its dinner. Taking a firm grip with the rear sucker, a place of contact is found and the leech probes with its forward sucker.

Fine, separated lips open to reveal a fantastic triangular set of jaws. Each of the three membranous pads, shaped like a half moon, is equipped with fifty or more microscopic teeth. Back-and-forth rotary motions of the jaws quickly produce three tiny incisions made so painlessly that they are seldom noticed unless the leech is watched at its work.

Through the pierced skin, vital fluids of its victim begin flowing down the leech's throat. Agitation of jaw muscles pumps a salivary chemical, hirudin, into the open wound to prevent coagulation. Few American leeches draw more than one sixth ounce of blood; European ones take three to six times as much.

Instead of a sack-like stomach, the leech has an extensive system of lobed compartments—usually nine or ten pairs of them. Even while the sucking of blood is in progress, liquid components of the meal are discharged through kidneys and skin; this keeps the animal wet, safeguards its fluid environment if feeding above surface. Only solid fractions from blood are retained and stored.

Circulated within the human system, red blood cells have a "working life" of only a few weeks. Packed into one of twenty storage sacs inside the leech's body, human cells are retained fresh for months. Gorged from a single feeding, the bloodsucker empties one storage sac at a time and digests its contents. One big meal is sufficient for a year. Whether some natural preservative is secreted by the leech is unknown. Philippine varieties are known to retain the virus of rinderpest alive for at least twenty-five days.

Glutted with blood from a human or four-footed animal, the leech is not only fortified to go for months without another meal; it is also ready to increase the population.

A true hermaphrodite, each leech has a complete set of both male and female organs. No individual fertilizes itself, however. Instead, it gives its sperm to a mate—and from the same or a different partner receives sperm which serve to fertilize its own eggs. After this has been accomplished, a dozen or more pale yellow eggs are wrapped in a cocoon whose end is closed with a temporary plug. Deposited in soil near the borders of a marsh, eggs hatch and release young leeches who push the plug from their cocoon and swim in search of food.

No matter where they may grow up, these prowlers have

relatively few dangerous enemies. Yellow perch and lake trout are fond of them, but most water creatures leave them alone. Except for polar zones, mountain peaks, and deserts, distribution is practically world-wide.

Even freezing doesn't thin leech ranks; temperatures must drop to 20° F. before they die. Most of them in temperate zones spend their winters in dormant states, are roused by the rising temperatures of spring. Drouth isn't necessarily fatal. Burrowing into mud and building a mucus-lined cell, an adult can survive four or five weeks without water.

No longer deliberately reared, leeches maintain populations in many regions. They constitute a minor nuisance on some fresh-water beaches, and are a source of considerable annoyance to cattle of Asia and the Philippines. Though vertebrate blood is preferred for the pre-mating feast, it is not essential. In a pinch, new generations can be reared from the blood of frogs and turtles. All these factors suggest that there is no likelihood of global extinction.

Though rather widely used in many regions of Asia, the animals are now sold in only a few drugstores of big Western cities. Some specialists regard them as unmatched for treatment of dental abscesses, and they drain black eyes so deftly that professional boxers are likely to insist upon having them.

Such easy demands do not challenge the species. Few today can pull rank by boasting of the notables on whom they have feasted. But descendants of Revolutionary soldiers aren't a fraction so numerous as pond dwellers who can pride themselves that blood of kings and rulers fed their ancestors.

Index

Adams, John, 207
Addax, 21
Alpaca, 15, 16, 22, 83
American Acclimatization Society, 25
American Museum of Natural History, 26
Anesthetic, cobra venom as, 78–79; discovered, 82; used in research, 82
Ant, 190, 225, 226, 227; carpenter, 224, 227; Kelep, 189; white (termite), 201
Anteater, Australian, 146
Antelope, 20
Antitoxin, developed, 82, 87, 88; produced in animals, 83; *see also* Serum
Apes, anthropoid, 230–44; compared with man, 241–42; described, 240, 241; early specimens sent to cities, 231; first historical mention, 231; range of, 243; *see also* Evolution
Aphid, 162, 165, 167
Arkwright, Sir Richard, 186
Asp, 75
Ass, domestication of, 15, 16; labor of, 22; as laboratory animal, 85; milk of, 19, 148, 149, 150; *see also* Hybridization
Auk, great, 210–11
Austin, Thomas, 213–14, 215
Australia, anteater of, 146; ladybirds from, 162–63; rabbit plague in, 213–22; starling in, 34; mentioned, 224

Babirussa, 173
Baden-Powell, Sir Robert, 171
Bat, 145, 198
Bear, American black, 195, 201; in art, 198–99; brown, 195, 198, 201; diet of, 194–96, 197, 200; in folklore and religion, 192–93, 194, 196–97, 198, 199; grizzly, 193, 195, 199–201; Kodiak, 195; and man, 193–94, 196, 197, 202, 230; polar, 193, 195, 199–201; prehistoric, 193, 197–99; red, 194; sloth, 201; taming of, 18
Beaver, 119
Bee, 43, 44; *see also* Honeybee
"Beebread," 45
Beetle, 224, 226; *see also* individual beetles
Beetle, squash, 167
Bible, 60, 70, 71, 72, 232, 237–38
Biology, founded and named, 232; some early theories of, 232–33
Birds, *see* individual birds
Bison, 17, 21, 132; *see also* Buffalo
Blackbird, 25, 32, 190
Bloodletting, *see* Leech
Boar, wild, 171–73; *see also* Pig
Boll weevil, Mexican, 181–91; damage by, 182, 189; diet of, 185; ecology of, 187, 189, 190–91; entry to U.S. of, 182, 188; impact on U.S. South of, 191; increase of, 187, 188–89; life cycle of, 183–85; war on, 189–91
Breeding, selective, 17, 18, 37, 149, 156–57, 159, 178–79, 234; *see also* Hybridization, and individual animals
Brewer, E. C., 37
Brunton, Sir T. Lauder, 87
Buffalo, conservation of, 117, 120; described, 112–13, 114; extinction

Buffalo (*cont'd*)
of, 117, 119, 120, 121, 125, 199; range of, 113–15, 117; and red man, 115–16, 120; uses of, 115–16, 118–19; wastage of, 117, 119; and white man, 116–17, 119, 120
Buffalo, water, 15, 16, 19, 22, 150
Butterfly, monarch, 33
Buzzard, 216

Cambyses II of Persia, 39
Camel, 16, 19, 22, 148, 149, 150, 217, 233
Canary, 21, 25, 31
Caribou, 21, 123, 200
Cat, *passim;* domestication of, 16, 18, 20; honored in England, 40; as hunter, 38, 41, 104; as laboratory animal, 85, 86, 87, 89; legend of origin, 36; in religious art, 37; reversion to wild state, 37–38; sacred in Egypt, 18, 37, 39, 42; selective breeding of, 18, 37; in superstition, 40, 41; as symbol of evil, 40; *tapetum lucidum* of, 41
Cattle, *passim;* domestication of, 14, 15, 16; hybridization of, 21; produce of, 22, 180; selective breeding of, 17, 37 (*see also* Cattle, dairy); as wolf prey, 123, 125–26, 132
Cattle, beef, 17, 169, 176, 191
Cattle, dairy; brought to New World, 149; chemistry of milk production in, 150–51; feeding of, 157; as principal source of dairy products, 149–50, 159–60; revered, 147; selective breeding of, 19, 149, 156–57, 159; tuberculosis in, 155–56; yield, 17, 150; *see also* Milk
Cavy, *see* Guinea pig
Centaur, 15, 73, 79
Centipede, 33, 140
Chaffinch, 26
Chamois, 21
Charles III of Spain, 64, 65
Chicken, 14, 16, 17, 22; *see also* Fowl
Chimpanzee, *see* Apes, anthropoid
Christianity, *see* Religion
Clay, Henry, 65, 179
Cobra, described, 73–75; hooded, 73–74; king, 72, 74, 75, 76, 77; range of, 73, 74, 75; religious significance of, 71, 72, 75; as sign of nobility, 71; "spitting," 75; *see also* Venom
Cod, by-products of, 211–12; commerce in, 204–7; conservation of, 210; described, 207–8, 209; diet of, 208; economic value of, 203, 204–7, 210; life cycle of, 208–9; medicinal use of, 211–12; natural enemies of, 209–10; political impact of, 207, 212
Codex Sinaiticus, 238
Colorado potato beetle, adaptability of, 95–96; destructiveness of, 92–93; diet of, 92, 99–100; insecticides and, 94, 97, 98–99 (*see also* DDT); in international politics, 90–91, 98; life cycle of, 95; named, 91; natural enemy, 33; spread of, 92–93, 96, 97; war on, 93–94, 96, 97, 98, 99
Coral snake, 77
Corn borer, 227
Cortés, Hernando, 13, 112, 175
Cotton, 181–91; economic importance of, 185–86, 187–88; history of, 185–86; machinery for, 186, 187–88; range of, 186–87, 188; *see also* Boll weevil
Cow, *see* Cattle, dairy
Coyote, 15
Crossbreeding, *see* Breeding, selective, and Hybridization
Crow, 31
Curie, Pierre, 82

Dairy products, *see* Milk
Darwin, Charles, 86, 234–37, 239, 243
DDT, discovered, 98; resistance to, 141; use of, 98–99, 140–41; *see also* Insecticides
Dead Sea Scrolls, 238
Deer, 18, 60, 123
Ditmars, Raymond L., 70, 74
Dog, *passim;* domestication of, 14–15, 23; as hunter, 104, 127, 132, 200; labor of, 22, 41; as laboratory animal, 85, 86; origin of, 15, 131;

Dog (*cont'd*)
selective breeding of, 17, 37, 132, 233; *see also* Breeding, selective
Dolphin, 146
Domestication of animals, 13–23; geography of, 16, 19, 22; history of, 14–16, 18, 22, 23; modifications due to, 17 (*see also* Breeding, selective, and Hybridization); purposes of, 21–22; theories of, 17–20, 21; *see also* individual animals
Donkey, *see* Hybridization
Dragonfly, 140
Drake, Sir Francis, 63, 207
Duck, 22, 23, 233

Eagle, 111
East India Company, 174
Ecology, man's impact on, *passim;* 16–17, 55–57, 94, 111, 116–19, 139–40, 164, 181, 187–90, 210–11, 213–14, 218, 220–21
Egypt, ancient, domestication of animals, 15, 17, 18, 19; religious significance of snake, 70, 71, of cattle and milk, 147; reverence for cat and pig, 18–19, 174; selective breeding of dairy cattle, 19
Elephant, 16, 22, 76, 124, 145
Elk, 123, 132, 195, 201
Essay on the Principle of Population, 234
Evolution, controversy over, 236–44; current theories of, 243–44; early theories of, 233–34; natural selection, 235; survival of the fittest, 234; *see also* Darwin, Charles, and Huxley, Thomas

Ferret, 104, 111, 216
Finch, 21
Flea, 103, 221
Flicker, 28, 32
Fly, 163; *see also* Fruit fly, Housefly, Sand fly
Fowl, domestication of, 14, 15; introduced to New Zealand, 25; produce of, 22; selective breeding of, 17, 37; used in sacred rites, 18; *see also* individual fowl
Fox, 177, 200, 214, 216, 219
Fruit fly, in research, 86

Galen, Claudius, 148, 248
Galton, Sir Francis, 21
Gazelle, 20
Geese, domestic, produce of, 22; white, sacred, 18; *see also* Fowl
Germ theory of disease, *see* Pasteur, Louis
Gibbon, 244
Giraffe, 233
Goat, domestication of, 16; milk of, 19, 147, 148, 150; produce of, 22
Goldfinch, 25
Gorilla, *see* Apes, anthropoid
Grackle, 27, 32
Grasshopper, 125
Greece, ancient, *passim;* centaur legend in, 15, 73; first use of serpent as symbol of healing, 73; religious rites to flies, 134, to cattle and milk, 147–48; reverence for serpent in, 71, 72; wolf lore of, 123, 128
Greene, Dr. M. B., 78
Grouse, 125
Guinea fowl, 15
Guinea pig, described, 83, 84; domestication of, 16; as food, 22, 83, 84; as laboratory animal, 80, 83–89; as pet, 84; *see also* Laboratory animals, and Research, medical

Hargreaves, James, 186
Harvey, William, 82
Hawk, 219
Heron, 111
Herring, 204
Hinny, 60–61; *see also* Mule
Hippocrates, 148
Hippopotamus, 246, 247
Historic Notebook, 37
Hog, 14, 17, 22; *see also* Pig
Hog, African forest, 173
Honey, commercial, 55; production of, 54; properties of, 54–55; *see also* Honeybee
Honeybee, commercial use of, 54–57; drone, 48, 49, 51; honey production of, 54; life cycle of, 44–46; "nectar dance" of, 52; nectar

Honeybee (*cont'd*)
gathering, 47, 54, 55; "nuptial flight" of, 49; physical adaptation for function, 46; pollen gathering, 47, 53, 55; pollination by, 53, 55–56; queen, 46, 47, 48, 49, 50, 51; royal jelly, 46, 50; as social insect, 43, 50, 52; specialization of labor, 43, 45, 46; survival of winter, 51–52
Horse, *passim;* in art, 199; *vs.* buffalo, 116, 117, 119; domestication of, 15, 16; hybridization of, 58 *et seq.;* labor of, 22, 180; as laboratory animal, 77, 85, 88; in legend, 15; milk of, 19, 150; produce of, 22; as religious sacrifice, 18; selective breeding of, 17, 37
Housefly, 133–43; as benefactor, 142; described, 136–37, 142; diet of, 136–37, 139; as disease bearer, 134–35, 136, 143; life cycle of, 137–38, 142–43; in military losses, 135; natural enemies of, 139–40; resistance to chemicals, 142; war on, 98, 135, 140–42
Howard, L. O., 134
Huxley, Thomas H., 210, 230, 236–37, 238–39, 240–41, 242, 243
Hybridization: of bison with cattle, 21; of jackass with mare, *see* Mule; of stallion with female donkey, 60, 61
Hyena, 21

Ibex, 21
India, *passim;* death rate by snake bite in, 76, 88, by plague in, 103; milk production in, 157, 158; snake in religions of, 70–71, 72, 75; wolf lore of, 129–30
Insecticides, 94, 97–99, 140–42; *see also* DDT
Insects, *see* individual insects

Jackal, 131, 177
Jackass, *see* Hybridization
Japanese beetle, 33
Jellyfish, blue, 209
Jenner, Edward, 87
Journal of Researches, 235
Judaism, *see* Religion
Jungle fowl, 17; *see also* Breeding, selective

Kangaroo, 213
Keen, Dr. William W., 80, 86
Koch, Robert, 84–85
Koebele, Albert, 162–63
Krait, 76

Laboratory animals, 14; controversy over use of, 80, 81, 85, 86; in medical research, 80 *et seq.* (*see also* Research, medical); protection of, 85–86; *see also* individual animals
Ladybird, 161–68; as benefactor, 161, 163–64, 165, 168; commerce in, 168; described, 165, 167; diet of, 166, 167; in folklore, 164, 166; impact on agriculture of, 164; imported to U.S., 163; as malefactor, 167; names of, 161, 164–65
Ladybug, *see* Ladybird
Lamarck, J. B., father of "biology," 232; theory of organic change, 233
Lamb, *see* Sheep
Leech, medicinal, 245–55; commerce in, 250–52; described, 252–53, 254; diet of, 253; history of use of, 246, 248–52; life cycle of, 254; purposes and methods of use of, 249–50; range of, 255
Leeuwenhoek, Anton van, 151
Leopard, 18, 21, 171, 172
Lightfoot, Dr. John, 232
Lion, 18, 171, 195, 201
Lizard, 18, 33, 139
Llama, 15, 16, 22, 83
Louse, as typhus carrier, 103

McCollum, E. V., 211
Magpie, 25
Malthus, Thomas, 234, 235
Mammals, characteristics of, 145; compared, 145–46; *see also* individual mammals, and Milk
Mammoth, 114, 169, 197, 199
Man, origin of, early theories about, 230, 231–33, 238; *see also* Evolution

Man's Place in Nature, 239
Martin, 33
Meadow lark, 190
Medicine, in Greek myth, 73; research in, *see* Research, medical
Mexican bean beetle, 167
Milk, 144–60; breeding for, 17, 19, 149, 156–57, 159; chemistry of, 151, 152, 153, 159; commercial distribution of, 156; commercial production of, 156–57; dangers of, 154–56; homogenization of, 151–52; human, 152–53; man's use of non-human, 146 *et seq.;* medicinal value of, 148, 152–53; packaging of, 157–58; pasteurization of, 154, 158–59; products, 148, 149, 155, 158, 160; in religious rites, 147–48; sources of, 19, 148–49, 150, 156–57, 159–60; in world nutrition, 158–59; *see also* Cattle, dairy, and Mammals
Mink, 119
Mongoose, 216
Monkey, as laboratory animal, 85, 88
Moose, 18, 195
Moslemism, *see* Religion
Mosquito, 221
Mouse, 77, 89, 145
Mueller, Paul, 1948 Nobel Prize winner in medicine for DDT, 98–99
Mule, butt of humor, 58, 59, 67; in development of New World, 63–67; as draft animal, 60, 61; hybrid of jackass and mare, 58, 59; as laboratory animal, 85; military use of, 60, 64, 65, 66, 67; as mount, 60, 62; as pack animal, 59, 60, 61, 62; Spanish controversy over, 62–63; special qualities of, 59; sterility of, 58; U.S. production of, 65–66; as West Point mascot, 66; mentioned, 230
Myna, 24

Neanderthal man, 197, 238, 239, 243
Nightingale, 26

Old Testament, *see* Bible
"On the Natural History of the Man-like Apes," 240–41
Opossum, 222
Orangutan, *see* Apes, anthropoid
Origin of Species, 236, 237, 239, 240
Oryx, 21
Owl, 111, 216, 219
Ox, domestication of, 15; labor of, 22; musk, 114; produce of, 22; wild, 114, 197, 199

Parrot, 25
Partridge, 31
Pasteur Institute, 77, 85, 221
Pasteur, Louis, and germ theory of disease, 87, 154, 160, 246; impact on development of serums and antitoxins, 87; and pasteurization, 154; and rabies serum, 82
Peccary, 21, 173
Peking man, 243
Pelican, white, 31
Pewee, 31
Pheasant, 25
Pig, 169–80; commercial production of, 176 *et seq.;* described, 170–71; diet of, 169–70, 172–73, 176; domestication of, 15, 16, 17, 19, 172–74, 177–78; as food, 169, 174, 175, 176, 180; imported to New World, 175; in religion, 18–19, 174; selective breeding of, 178–79
Pigeon, 22, 77; carrier, 42; passenger, 17
Pipit, 190
Plague, bubonic, 102–4, 134
Plant louse, *see* Aphid
Pork, *see* Pig
Potato bug, *see* Colorado potato beetle
Poultry, 176, 216; *see also* Fowl
Praying mantis, 140
Ptarmigan, 31, 125
Punch, on evolution, 237

Rabbit, in Australia, 213–22; commerce in, 219; damage by, 214, 215, 218, 219, 220; diet of, 215; fecundity of, 178, 214–15; in folklore, 219; as food, 213, 218, 219; as game, 213, 214, 219; as labora-

Rabbit (*cont'd*)
tory animal, 84, 89, 220; milk of, 146, 152; myxomatosis in, 220–22; natural enemies of, 125, 216, 219; produce of, 219; war on, 214, 215–17, 219, 220–22
Rat, diet of, 106, 108; as disease bearer, 101, 102–4; increase of, 110, 111; intelligence of, 108, 109–10; spread of, 102, 104–6; teeth of, 107; vandalism of, 102, 106, 107–8, 219; war on, 102, 104, 106, 110–11
Rat, black, 102, 103, 105; brown, 103, 104–6; gray, 109; white, as laboratory animal, 86, 107, 108, 110; *see also* Rat
Rats, Lice, and History, 103
Rattlesnake, 77, 79, 169; *see also* Snake
Redshank, 31
Reindeer, American, 21; in art, 199; domestication of, 16; milk of, 19, 147, 150
Religion, *passim; see also* individual animals and religions
Religion, Buddhist, 70–71, 72; Christian, 18, 62, 63, 148, 232, 237 (*see also* Bible); Hindu, 70–71, 72; Jewish, 60, 72, 174, 237 (*see also* Bible); Moslem, 62, 63, 174
Religious art, bear in, 198; cat figures in Egyptian graves, 37; serpent (cobra) in, 70, 71
Religious ritual, current, with cobra, 75–76; dedicated to flies, 134; dissection of fowl, 18; interment of animals in burial mounds, 19; with milk, 147–48; Roman use of cobra in, 72; sacrifice of horse, 18
Religious significance: of bear, 193, 196; of cat, 18, 37; of pig, 174; of serpent (cobra), 70, 71, 72, 75–76; of white geese, 18
Religious taboos, on milking, 19; on use of pig, 18, 174
Reptiles, 233; *see also* individual reptiles
Research, medical, control and legal restriction of, 85–86; in drugs and foods, 88; guinea pig in, 83, 84, 85; on human subjects, involuntary, 81; in public health, 87, 88–89; by self-experimentation, 81–82; surgical experiments in, 85, 87; use of anesthetics and antiseptics in, 82; in uses of snake venom, 77–79; using laboratory animals, 80 *et seq.* (*see also* Laboratory animals)
Rhinoceros, woolly, 114, 197, 199
Richter, Dr. Curt P., 108
Riley, C. V., 93, 162, 182
Ringhal, 74
Robin, 31, 32
Rodents, 85, 145, 146; *see also* individual rodents
Rome, ancient, *passim;* mule-breeding in, 60, 61; regard for serpent in, 71, 72; reverence for pig in, 174; sacred white geese of, 18; wolf legend of, 129

Salmon, 196, 204
Sand fly, 221
Say, Thomas, and Colorado potato beetle, 91; "father of American entomology," 91
Scale insect, 161–62, 163, 167
Schieffelin, Eugene, 25, 26
Seal, 146, 200
Sepoy Mutiny, 174
Serpent, *see* Snake
Serum, anthrax, 87; diphtheria, 87; myxomatosis, 221; rabies, 82, 88; smallpox, 87; snake-bite, 77; spinal meningitis, 88; tetanus, 88; yellow fever, 87; *see also* Pasteur Institute, and Pasteur, Louis
Shark, 203
Sheep, *passim;* anthrax in, 87; Australian, 34, 215, 216, 217; domestication of, 14, 15, 16, 17; milk of, 19, 148, 149, 150; produce of, 17, 22, 176, 180; as wolf prey, 123, 126, 132
Silkworm, 56
Skylark, 25, 26
Sloth, ground, 114
Snail, 33
Snake, 68–79; in Bible, 70; cults, 72,

Snake (*cont'd*)
73, 75–76; eating habits of, 74, 111; as fertility symbol, 71, 72, 75; harmless species of, 68; as immortality symbol, 70, 72; locomotion of, 68–69; molting of, 69; in myth and legend, 70, 71, 72–73; in religious art, 70; religious significance of, 70 *et seq.;* as sexual symbol, 71; as symbol of healing, 68, 72–73; tongue of, 70; venom of, 68, 76–79; *see also* individual snakes, and Venom
Snake bite, death rate in Asia, 76; serum, 77; *see also* Venom
Snout beetle, *see* Weevil
Sparrow, hedge, 25; house, 35
Spider, 33, 139
Squid, giant, 203
Stalin, Joseph, 245
Starling, European, courtship and mating of, 32–33; described, 26, 31; diet of, 33–34; as food, 35; imported to U.S., 26; migration of, 32; as mimic, 28, 31–32; nesting habits, 32, 34; as pest, 25, 27, 29, 30; as pet, 25, 28; speech of, 24–25, 31–32; spread of, 27–30; war on, 30–31, 35
Stork, 111
Superstitions, about cats, 40; about snakes, 70
Swallow, 33
Swine, *see* Pig

Tapeti, 220
Tapir, 114
"Tendency of Varieties to Depart Infinitely from the Original Type," 236
Termite, 201
Thrush, song, 26
Tick, 34
Tiger, 124, 195
Titmouse, 190
Toad, 139
Turkey, domestic, 15, 16, 23
Turtle, giant, 234
Typhoid fever, 135, 155
Typhus, 102, 103, 104

Venom, snake, antidote to, 87–88; composition of, 76–77; hemotoxic, 77; medicinal use of, 68, 77–79; neurotoxic, 77; toxicity of, 76; varying reactions to, 77; *see also* Snake
Viper, 76; Russell's, 79
Vivisection, *see* Research, medical
Vulture, 111, 126

Wallace, Alfred Russell, 235–36
Walrus, 114, 200
Wart hog, 173
Wasp, 44, 140
Water buffalo, *see* Buffalo, water
Water moccasin, 77
Weasel, 104, 111, 216, 219
Weevil, 33, 182; *see also* Boll weevil
Whale, 145, 146, 203
Whitney, Eli, 42, 187
Wildcat, 36, 175
Wolf, compared to dog, 124–25; contribution of, 131–32; described, 124; diet of, 125, 126; in folklore, 123–24, 126, 127–30; *vs.* man, 122–23, 125–26, 130–31, 132; as man-eater, 126–27; range of, 122
Wood louse, 33
Woodpecker, 32, 224; ivorybill, 224, 225, 226; *see also* Woodpecker, pileated
Woodpecker, pileated, adaptation of, 227–28; as benefactor, 229; damage by, 223, 228, 229; described, 224, 225–26; diet of, 224, 227; range of, 224; war on, 224–25, 228–29
Wren, 190

Yak, 19
Yellow jacket, 44, 195; *see also* Wasp

Zebra, 21
Zebu, 16, 19
Zinsser, Hans, 103